Our Place in the Universe: Judaism and the Environment

Lesson Plan Manual

By Marc Rosenstein, Tova Sacher, and Sigalit Ur
Galilee Foundation for Value Education

BEHRMAN HOUSE

Behrman House, Inc.
www.behrmanhouse.com/universe

When God created the first humans, God took them and showed them all the trees of paradise and said: See My works, how beautiful and perfect they are! Everything I have created, I created for you. Take care that you do not spoil and destroy My world, for if you do, there is no one to repair it for you.

—*Midrash Kohelet Rabbah 7:13*

Much of the material in this book was originally prepared by the authors for internal use at Bialik College, Melbourne, Australia. The authors and publisher are grateful to Bialik College for granting permission to adapt this material for a larger audience.

Design: AURAS Design
Project editor: Dena Neusner
Editorial consultants: Ellen Bernstein, Ellen Rank

Springfield, New Jersey 07081
www.behrmanhouse.com

ISBN 978-0-87441-911-5
Printed in the United States of America

Visit www.behrmanhouse.com/universe for more resources.

Contents

Introduction

Why Teach the Environment from a Jewish Perspective?

A central goal of Jewish education is to help our students find, in the classical sources of our tradition, moral guidance as they face the dilemmas of life in the modern world. If Judaism is to be more than just ethnic identity or a collection of quaint customs, we must continue the eternal process of interpreting and applying its beliefs, laws, and stories, to find in them relevance to our own life situation.

In recent decades, the growing impact of humanity on the natural universe and the growing awareness of that impact have brought questions of environmental morality to the center of attention throughout Western society, in education, politics, economics, art, etc. Therefore, we as Jewish educators must ask: What guidance can Judaism offer us in dealing with these questions?

In fact, humanity's relationship to the natural world has been a concern of Judaism from our earliest texts. It is possible to see the entire beginning of the Torah—the Creation, the expulsion from Eden, Noah, the Tower of Babel—as a series of attempts to find the balance between our right to exploit the world and our responsibility to take care of it. And this concern is not limited to the formative myths of Genesis but continues to be addressed by the Torah and its interpreters throughout the generations.

Therefore, we don't have to dig too deep or stretch too far to find guidance from our tradition as we address current dilemmas relating to conservation, consumption, environmental quality, and intervention in natural processes. There are multiple opportunities to connect our classical texts with our students' real-life experiences.

It is tempting, in teaching about Judaism and the environment, simply to take commonly accepted environmental positions and seek Jewish support, or proof texts, for them. However, this would be an oversimplification. If we want our students to be thoughtful about difficult dilemmas and to seek answers in Jewish sources then it is important not to preach to them, but to help them grapple with these dilemmas in the light of the sources.

For example, the classic dichotomy of Genesis 1:28 ("fill the earth and master it...") versus Genesis 2:15 ("to till and to tend...") informs all subsequent discussions: What is our place as humans in this world? Are we here to rule over it and exploit it since we are the pinnacle of Creation? Or were we placed at the pinnacle of knowledge and sensitivity in order to understand that we are to be awed by the world and responsible for its well-being and its very survival? Or is the answer, perhaps, more nuanced than either of these approaches?

These are the questions that come back again and again, with respect to air and water, endangered species, nuclear power, genetic engineering, vegetarianism, and so on. When to intervene in nature, and how, are questions that are basic to every human enterprise, and to which Judaism has offered insights in many different time periods and contexts. Living in the real world requires us to constantly seek the right balance.

The goal of this series of lessons is to challenge the students to understand and think seriously about these dilemmas in a Jewish context, and to help them bring their Jewish commitments and knowledge to bear on their responses.

Handle with Care

Many of the topics discussed in this book are the center of contentious public debate and political conflict, in which scientific questions, morality, cost-benefit analyses, and personal interests can become hopelessly tangled up. These topics provide opportunities for each of us to question, debate, struggle, and form our own opinions. You can encourage a thoughtful approach by taking care to avoid simplistic answers and to be aware of your own biases. The purpose of the course is *not* to advocate for a specific position on vegetarianism, logging, or genetically engineered foods, for example. The goal is to help students think critically about these issues, and to take into account insights from Jewish texts, ideas, and practices as they formulate their own positions.

Structure of the Course

The course comprises seven chapters of two or three lessons each. Each chapter deals with an important theme or topic relating to humanity's relationship with the world around us. Here is an overview of the course:

Chapter 1: Stories We Tell about the World: This chapter examines formative myths from the Torah. We will look at the Creation stories and the Tower of Babel, and how these stories articulate ambivalence regarding our place in the universe. Are we masters or caretakers? Is the world ours or are we part of it?

Chapter 2: Nature in Jewish Laws and Customs: This chapter explores several *mitzvot* that reflect our relationship to nature: the reciting of blessings, *b'rachot,* as a symbol of our appreciation; the principal of *bal tashchit* ("do not destroy"), found in the Torah; and the commandments of Shabbat and *sh'mitah*, that limit our freedom to exploit nature.

Chapter 3: The Animal Kingdom: The creations closest to humans are animals, and we have an ambivalent relationship to them; even as we exploit them, we feel sympathy for them. We'll take a macro look—what obligation do we have to prevent extinction of species—and a micro look—what do our sources teach about cruelty and kindness to animals?

Chapter 4: Sharing Public Resources: The classic Talmudic distinction between private and public space turns out to be a key concept in discussions of individuals' (and corporations') responsibility for managing shared resources. We will study the general principle of "the commons," and examine a case study: water conservation.

Chapter 5: Our Responsibility to the Future: An important theme in current environmental discourse is, how much must we sacrifice our own comfort and quality of life for the sake of unborn generations? The first lesson addresses the definition of "quality of life" and its relationship to consumption. The next two lessons focus on the specific phenomenon of climate change and how we can respond to it.

Chapter 6: Setting Limits: In the past, tampering with nature meant building a dam on a river; today it can mean raising the level of all the oceans. We will examine two cases of deep human intervention in natural processes, nuclear energy and genetic engineering, and discuss whether we have the obligation to set limits on these interventions, and how to know where to draw the line.

Chapter 7: Striking the Right Balance: In this chapter we'll examine a case study of intervention in nature in Israel, with special attention to the problem of unintended consequences; and we will look at impressive and inspiring examples of current Jewish environmental pioneering. Finally, we'll try to synthesize and prioritize the various values encountered in all the preceding chapters in order to help students to move from knowledge to action.

Structure of the Lessons

Each lesson plan relates directly to content in the *Our Place in the Universe Journal*, and includes:

- **Central Questions**: Driving questions that reflect the main ideas of the lesson
- **Goals**: Objectives that students will achieve by the end of the lesson
- **Introduction**: A brief introduction to the topic for the teacher, with background information as needed
- **Materials Needed**
- **Activities**: Step-by-step directions for presenting the lesson, including discussion topics, hands-on activities, and individual and group work
- **Enrichment Options**: Optional activities, projects, and even puzzles for further exploration and study. These include suggestions for individual or class projects that allow the students to explore concepts more deeply, demonstrate their understanding, and/or apply their learning through action
- **Further Resources**: Suggestions both for the teacher's own reference, and for materials and activities for classroom use

The lessons are each designed to be taught in one class period of 45 to 50 minutes. However, many lessons can be expanded into two or more class periods if the teacher and the class are interested, using the supplementary materials, ideas, and group projects suggested in the **Enrichment Options** section in each lesson.

On the other hand, it is possible to shorten the course by selecting a limited number of lessons, such as by choosing one lesson from each chapter, or by choosing only those chapters that most interest you and the class. In general, the chapters and the lessons are not sequential: it is not necessary to first cover material in the earlier lessons in order to be prepared for the later ones. The only exceptions might be chapter 1, which serves as an introduction to the whole course, and lesson 17, which is intended as a wrap-up or summation.

Practical Suggestions for the Teacher

Using the Journal: The journal is an essential part of this course and directly corresponds to the material in this Lesson Plan Manual. Each chapter of the journal opens with a journaling activity, to give students the opportunity to bring their own experiences and reflections to the topic. You may want to use discussion of these written entries to introduce the issues to be addressed in the new chapter.

For each lesson, this Lesson Plan Manual suggests overall goals and specific activities, with rough time allocations. The journal provides trigger and wrap-up activities, and the text passages and study questions needed to carry out the activities suggested in the Lesson Plan Manual. The journal is not an independent-study workbook. The activities and materials in it are designed to fit the larger context of the lesson as presented in the Lesson Plan Manual. It is a tool to make life easier for the teacher and to provide an interesting and interactive resource for classroom use —but it is not meant to replace the complete lesson plan.

Note that there are different ways to use the journal:

- You can give students time to work independently on particular text passages or written assignments, and then reconvene and share their results. If your school culture allows for homework, you can ask students to do these assignments outside of class. If not, then it is probably best to keep the books in the classroom, to make sure they are there when you need them.
- You can let students work in small groups or pairs, and then reconvene and share.
- You can read the text passages together as a class and use them and the attendant discussion questions as a basis for class discussion, without writing.
- When students are given time to work on texts or exercises independently, the puzzle feature can productively occupy the time of those who finish ahead of the rest of the class.

Journaling: Note that the journal contains a number of opportunities for journaling. This is an important tool for individualizing instruction, and for helping students find their own connections between the content of the class and the reality of their own lives. Encourage students to express themselves freely: they can draw or write; and they don't need to worry about presentation, as the journal is their own private place and sharing will always be optional. An important benefit of journaling is to give every student a chance for expression, even those who don't comfortably speak out in class.

Classroom Debate: Holding a formal debate can be a useful technique to encourage students to think critically about difficult dilemmas. The key elements of a classroom debate are:

- A clear statement that can be argued for or against.
- Teams assigned to the pro and con positions without respect for students' personal views.
- A structured, enforced schedule, with opening statements by each side, followed by alternating rebuttals.
- A requirement that arguments, at least in the opening statements, be explicitly based on sources—facts or statements by authorities.

If you hold a vote after the debate, be careful to provide structured judging guidelines based on the issues and supporting authorities, so as to avoid a popularity contest.

Scanning the Media: Almost every day, television, the internet, social media, and newspapers present new information about environmental issues, including new dilemmas, new problems, and new solutions. Be on the lookout for materials that may be relevant to particular lessons in the course, and encourage your students, as well, to bring relevant news items to class for discussion in the context of the values and texts presented in the lessons.

Environmental Ideas Corner: Consider setting aside a corner of the classroom, a section of a bulletin board, or a page on the school website, to which you and the students can contribute news items, ideas, and visuals that relate to the various topics in the course. This area might also include practical suggestions that arise from the class (e.g., recycling the water from the drain of the drinking fountain; doing all written assignments by e-mail without printing; posting instructions for composting).

Thinking Green: Think about ways to raise the environmental consciousness of the class by means of your own day-to-day management: reusing paper, turning off lights, being conscious of waste in heating and air conditioning.

Community Awareness: Consider bringing in guest speakers from the community, whether professionals or laypeople, who are knowledgeable about environmental action projects. Field trips are also a possibility: the class could survey waste-promoting packaging in a supermarket, tour a landfill or recycling facility, or explore conflicts between development and nature conservation in your area.

Environmental Action Projects: Most lessons include suggestions for action projects, to encourage students to apply their learning to practical environmental issues in their homes and community. These project ideas (or other ideas that they inspire) can be used to enrich learning in a few different ways:

- **Independent projects**: Individual students or small groups may be interested in particular projects and decide to take them on independently. If they do, be sure to allow time in class for them to report on their progress and results.
- **Project based learning**: You might choose to use a project as the core method for addressing the lesson topic, instead of (or in addition to) the suggested lesson activities. Consider creating a project based learning experience, where the students lead their own inquiries, and learn by researching and by doing. They might conduct research in the community and/or on the Internet to pursue a topic about which they are curious, and they might create a product (booklet, video, slide show, bulletin board, community action project) that demonstrates their understanding and educates others on what they have learned. You can find more information on project based learning on page 64 of this book, or visit www.behrmanhouse.com/project-based-learning.
- **Digital resources**: The Internet is rich with information about the field of environmental research and activism. You and your students can use a wide variety of digital resources to enhance your knowledge and spark new ideas on the content you're studying.

  You can start by visiting the course website (www.behrmanhouse.com/universe) regularly, for links to sites with particular relevance to the chapters of this book. However, the resources on this site are not exhaustive, and you and your students should be encouraged to use your own search skills and tools to explore the topics that interest you and share your learning with the class.

  Note that the Behrman House Online Learning Center offers a platform for sharing information and collaborating on projects. You can find more information about the Online Learning Center here: www.behrmanhouse.com/olc/discover-the-online-learning-center

  One way to demonstrate "green teaching" in this course is to minimize the use of paper handouts and maximize the use of digital presentations, like videos, slide shows, etc.

The *Our Place in the Universe* Game Pack: Encourage students to explore the free game pack that can be found at www.behrmanhouse.com/universe. The game pack includes crossword puzzles, personality quizzes, Mad Libs, and more, and provides a fun way to reinforce the themes presented in *Our Place in the Universe* at home or at school. Most of the games can be printed or played online.

CHAPTER

1

Stories We Tell About the World

Creation myths may not represent scientific truth, but they can give us important insight and guidance regarding our relationship to the natural world. For example, the existence of two different accounts of Creation in the first two chapters of Genesis sets up a dilemma that is the central theme of just about any discussion of our place in the universe; thus Lesson 1 is the indispensable introduction to any course on Judaism and the environment. Lesson 2 examines the environmental implications of technology in another biblical narrative, the story of the Tower of Babel.

As a preface to the first lesson, discuss with students how they feel about nature and their relationship as humans to the natural world. Invite them to write or draw their thoughts in the journal, page 6.

Lesson 1 — Nature and Our Creation Stories

Central Questions: As humans, what is our relationship to nature? Are we a part of nature, or are we above it?

Goals: Students will...

1. Explain that there is no single approach to the question of the place of humanity in nature, but rather that there are multiple, nuanced attitudes.
2. Reflect upon the effect of the Jewish Creation stories on our culture's view of nature.
3. Describe what is (or is not) unique about the biblical approach to nature.

Introduction

The first two chapters of the book of Genesis recount two very different stories of Creation. There have been many attempts, traditional and modern, to reconcile the stories. Some have even suggested that the Genesis 1 version ("fill the earth and master it") is responsible for a way of thinking that has led to our environmental crisis. But another approach suggests that the different accounts propose different attitudes, both of which have a place within Judaism, and that it's a question of balance. Other cultures may hold completely different views about the hierarchy of Creation.

Materials Needed

Bibles or photocopies of Genesis 1 and 2

Activities

1. Getting Started: In the Beginning (5 minutes)

Distribute to the class the Creation stories in Genesis (you can photocopy the relevant pages, or distribute copies of the Bible and show students how to find the chapters and verses): chapter 1, and chapter 2, verses 4-19.

As a class, review the first Creation account, using the **In the Beginning** exercise on page 7 of the journal. Alternatively, you could ask students to try this exercise at home prior to class, or have a competition in class to find the answers. *(Answers: Plants, day 3; Fish, day 5; Stars, day 4; Sky, day 2; Humans, day 6; Light, day 1; Dry land, day 3; Birds, day 5; Cattle, day 6; Sea creatures, day 5)*

2. Two Creation Stories (15 minutes)

Read the key passages (Genesis 1:24-31 and 2:4-19) aloud, and discuss: Did students ever notice before that there are two different Creation stories? How do we reconcile them? Is one of them the "true" story? (You might want to suggest that since the Torah offers two different stories, this shows that it does not seek to present scientific truth, but rather to suggest different ways in which we can see our place as humans in the universe.)

Give the students time, working on their own, to compare the two stories, using the chart in the journal, page 7. The chart is reproduced below with answers included. Use students' answers as the basis for a class discussion of the worldviews of the two stories.

	According to Genesis 1	**According to Genesis 2**
When were humans created, last or first?	*Last (from verses 26-27)*	*First (verse 7)*
What is humanity's relation to nature?	*Humans were created to rule over nature (verse 28: God blessed them and said to them, "Be fruitful and increase in number; fill the earth and master it. Rule over the fish in the sea and the birds in the sky and over every living creature that moves on the ground.")*	*Humans were created to take care of nature. (verse 15: God took the man and put him in the Garden of Eden to work it and take care of it.)*
Does nature need humans?	*No—before the middle of the sixth day the world functioned without humans (verses 20-25).*	*Yes—it seems that humans were needed to work the ground, so before their creation God did not create bushes or plants (verse 5: no bush of the field was yet in the land and no small plant of the field had yet sprung up—for God had not caused it to rain on the land, and there was no man to work the ground).*

Reconvene and compare notes. Try to help students see that the two stories imply worldviews that are very different. According to Genesis 1, humans were created last; this could imply that humans were the crowning glory of Creation, after God had made the whole world in preparation. In this view, humanity's mission is to fill the earth and subdue its creatures, all of whom have been created for our use and pleasure. Genesis 2 tells a different story—humans were created first so they could be in place to work the land and tend the world; our role as caretaker and keeper is stressed in this version.

Discuss briefly as preparation for the next section: Do students have a preference for one of the stories? Is one more ideal and one more real?

3. The Genesis Stories and Current Environmental Dilemmas (20 minutes)

Divide the students into four groups, and assign two groups to each environmental dilemma presented in the journal, page 8. For each dilemma, one group should consider the problem according to Genesis 1 ("fill the earth and master it") and the other group according to Genesis 2 ("work it and take care of it"). Give the students a few minutes to write down their individual responses; then let each group discuss their responses with each other and choose a spokesperson to present their thoughts to the whole class.

Encourage students to debate their views. You could do this as a formal debate: For each dilemma, a spokesman for the Genesis 1 group gets 3 minutes to present, and then the spokesman for Genesis 2 gets 3 minutes to rebut. Then there can be an orderly back and forth, with a one minute time limit, or you can just open up the discussion to everyone after the two initial presentations.

It is important to point out that the implications of the Creation stories are not as clear-cut as they may seem. The desired outcome of this exercise is to raise tough questions not answer them. Some of the specific dilemmas will come back in subsequent lessons, in more depth; here their purpose is just to serve as examples of how the two worldviews in Genesis interact.

Here are some possible responses to the dilemmas:

a. Should we hunt deer to prevent overpopulation?
   Genesis 1, "fill the earth and master it," seems to imply that man can bend the world to his needs; since deer are eating up our gardens and forests, this text implies that man may cull them. But if we listen to Genesis 2, "to work it and to take care of it," we have to question whether we may destroy part of nature for our own needs. And what if that part of nature is destructive in itself? For more on this topic, go to www.bloomberg.com and search "deer infestation."

b. Should people stop using cars to prevent global warming and preserve oil resources and green spaces?
   A Genesis 1 argument might stress the importance of cars for the necessities of life as well as for fun activities. But does this mean Genesis 1 would allow us to destroy the environment for our convenience? A Genesis 2 argument would point to the negative impacts of cars, from polluting the air, to using up nonrenewable resources, to paving over large amounts of land. But does Genesis 2 mean that we must put the environment above our own needs? And what if our car use in wealthy North America impacts cities in poor countries like Brazil?

4. Humans and the Natural World (10 minutes)

Discuss with students how other cultures have Creation stories that may reflect different views of the relationship between humans and the natural world. Ask students to look at the pictures and read the story in the journal (pages 9-10).

Discuss how the photos and story reflect the beliefs of these cultures. *(The cow is protected with a blanket and not tied up. This gentle treatment reflects the Hindu belief regarding the sacredness of cows. The monks of the Jain religion, also originating in India, take extraordinary steps to avoid harming animals, even by accident. The Creation story comes from Jicarilla Apache legend; the animals' role in the creation of humans expresses the belief that humans do not have dominion over animals but instead must respect them as partners in the world.)*

Conclude with a brief wrap-up, returning to the questions: Why does Genesis tell such disparate stories? Is there truth in both of them? How do we find the right balance? What can we learn from other cultures' stories?

Enrichment Options

WHAT WOULD THE WORLD LOOK LIKE? Ask students to imagine that two identical earths were created at the same time, with all the same creatures, climate, etc. However, on Earth 1, the people behaved only according to Genesis 1, while on Earth 2, the people behaved only according to Genesis 2. How would the two worlds be different? Students can describe their answer in words or illustrate it with drawings.

PROJECT BASED LEARNING: WHAT CAN I DO? Encourage students to identify a problem in their town or region related to one of the environmental issues in this lesson (animal overpopulation, car use). They should research it and think about these questions: What is the nature of the problem? How is it affecting the environment? What should be done about it? What can I do? Then students prepare a presentation and an action plan for responding to it in the community; for example, promoting public transportation or supporting an animal shelter. Encourage students to connect what they've learned in this lesson to the proposal.

Using student-driven goals and a real-life presentation, craft a project based learning activity around this topic. See page 64 for more information on project based learning, and also visit www.behrmanhouse.com/project-based-learning.

ORIGINAL CREATION STORY Students write or illustrate their own original Creation story, starting from what they believe about the place of humans in the universe, and expressing that belief in an interesting and colorful way. Ask students to imagine that their story was the defining Creation story for a nation. How would it affect the culture of the people who believed in it? You could add these original Creation stories to the exhibition of artwork suggested above. Alternatively, you could ask students to act out their own Creation stories.

Further Resources

Visit www.behrmanhouse.com/universe for links to an article about the two Creation stories and the environment, a collection of Creation stories from around the world, and more.

Lesson 2 — The Tower of Babel: The Perils of Progress

Central Questions: What fuels our urge for technological progress? What are the benefits of this progress? The dangers? The costs?

Goals: Students will…

1. Talk about the story of the tower of Babel and its message regarding the impact of technology on the world.
2. Discuss the benefits and dangers of technological development.

Introduction

Following the story of Noah's Ark, the book of Genesis relates the tale of the Tower of Babel. Mankind gathers together in one place and, after learning how to bake bricks, decides to embark on a grandiose building project—a tower that reaches the heavens. As work progresses, God brings the endeavor to an end by "confusing their languages" so that the builders can no longer understand each other and therefore are unable to continue working together. As a result the project is abandoned and the people then spread out and inhabit different lands. Is this a story about a historical event? An attempt to explain why there are different languages? Or perhaps, is it an expression of ambivalence regarding the impact of the human drive for technological advance? This last interpretation is the focus of this lesson.

Biblical commentators offer many different interpretations of the story of the Tower of Babel and explanations for what brought God to stop the project and scatter the people. Some try to identify the "sin" that brought about the punishment. But the verses themselves are neutral on the nature of the building. God's reaction is similarly not defined. God is neither angry nor pleased but rather predicts an unwanted outcome to the project and remedies the situation. Many understand the biblical story as a retelling of a historical event that is recorded in other sources of the time.

However it is possible to interpret the story on a metaphorical level. The image of humans building a tower to reach the heavens resonates in our times. Both physically and figuratively mankind has sought and succeeded to "reach the heavens." We have developed technology that has enabled us to harness and manipulate nature to serve our own needs and purposes. This on-going search for bigger and better technology has fueled humankind's progress, improving and enriching our lives in countless ways. At the same time this relentless progress has taken its toll on the environment: depleting resources, upsetting natural balances, and destroying unique landscapes. It has also had negative effects on individuals and human society, causing dehumanization, materialism, competition, war, and a world where the next technological advance has become an end unto itself.

Materials Needed

Construction supplies: tape, boxes, paper tubes, paper plates and cups, cartons, cardboard, straws, etc.

Activities

1. Getting Started: Why Build a Tower? (15 minutes)

Divide the class into groups of 5 to 7 students. Give each group a box or bag of simple construction supplies (tape, paper plates/cups, cardboard, straws, etc.). Give the groups 7 minutes to build whatever they want, with no guidance.

When the time is up, interview each group as they show their result:

- What was their goal in building their structure? Height? Strength? Beauty? Having fun together? Why did they do what they did?
- How did they make decisions together? Consensus? Voting? Loudest/strongest member(s)?
- Did they think they were competing with the other groups?

Use this experience to raise the question of why people build or invent new things; why don't they just keep living the way they always have? Is it always out of need? Are all of our buildings and inventions only what we need? What about beauty? Play? Pride? Competition? Is there a human need to be creative just for our own satisfaction, even when our physical needs don't require it? Do big building projects and technological challenges bring people together or pull them apart? Who benefits from the building projects?

2. The Tower of Babel (15 minutes)

Read the story of the Tower of Babel together in class (Genesis 11:1-9; in the journal, page 11). Stop often and ask the class to explain the verses to make sure they understand the story. You might want to point out Babylonia on a map.

Questions to raise:

- What is the new technology that allows the people in this story to think of a large tower?
- What is their goal?
- Is there anything wrong with this?
- Why does God intervene? Do you think this is right?
- Why does God choose this particular method of stopping them? Why not an earthquake, for instance?
- How would the world be different if all people spoke the same language?

3. Looking for Explanations (15 minutes)

Have students read the two commentaries on page 12 in the journal and choose the one they prefer. Discuss their responses. You might want to invite students to propose other explanations for why God stopped the tower from being built. Here are some notes on the commentaries:

a. *Pirkei D'Rabbi Eli'ezer* (a collection of explanations and retellings of biblical stories, dating to the 700s) argues that the builders lost sight of their humanity and cared more about the tower than about the workers. Challenge students to think of modern examples of this. For example, the conditions of factory workers in Asia who make clothing and electronics for us.

b. Isaac Abravanel (statesman and Bible commentator, Spain, Portugal, Italy, 1400s) suggests that the builders weren't satisfied with their lot; instead they were striving for bigger, fancier, and flashier.

Discuss: Does that ever happen in our day? For example: big cars and houses, and expensive clothes, as status symbols.

As an alternative, invite students to imagine a modern version of the Babel story. What other technological advances and obstacles, besides architecture and language, might be the focus of this story? (*for example, the Internet, space travel, cloning, nuclear power, fracking, Facebook)* What technological advances do you think may not be a good idea to continue? What obstacle might replace the scrambling of languages? Ask students to write or draw their stories, or perform them with a friend as a skit or video.

Enrichment Options

PUZZLE TIME: THE TOWER OF BABEL TODAY Students can work on matching the names to the pictures of modern day towers on page 13 if they have extra time individually or together as a class, or at home. Ask them to think of how the projects are similar to or different from the Tower of Babel. (*The similarities can be in the sheer size of the project, in the way it brings people together, or in how it exploits people or the environment.*) (Visit www.behrmanhouse.com/universe for links about the specific projects.)

Here are answers and some facts about the projects pictured:

1-c: Burj Khalifa (Khalifa Tower), Dubai, United Arab Emirates—the tallest man-made structure in the world, at 2,722 feet.

2-e: European Parliament Buildings, Strasbourg, France—according to (false) rumors, it was designed to look like the tower of Babel as it appears in a Renaissance painting.

3-a: Sydney Opera House, Sydney, Australia—took almost twenty years to build because the architect designed it before engineers had figured out how to build the shapes he wanted.

4-b: One World Trade Center (Freedom Tower), New York City—the tallest building in the Western Hemisphere at 1,776 feet, in reference to the year of American independence.

5-d: Three Gorges Dam, Yangtze River, China—the world's largest hydroelectric power station.

MY BABEL Have students create a drawing, painting, or three-dimensional model of the Tower of Babel, either from their own imagination or based on images created by artists in the past. Encourage them to decorate it with words and/or images indicating the benefits and dangers of technological progress. You could make a display of individual works, or do this as a group project.

REFLECTING ON CHAPTER 1 This lesson concludes chapter 1, which can be seen as the "philosophical" introduction to this course. This might be a good time to ask students to look back on the journaling exercise at the beginning of the chapter, regarding their relation to the natural world: What have they learned in these lessons that reflects or challenges what they wrote?

Further Resources

Visit www.behrmanhouse.com/universe for more information and pictures about the Tower of Babel, and about the modern towers featured in this lesson.

CHAPTER 2

Nature in Jewish Laws and Customs

One way to understand the relationship beteen humanity and nature in Jewish tradition is to examine formative myths, as we did in chapter 1. Another way is to study the laws and customs that govern that relationship. What are we required to do, or forbidden to do, in our treatment of the world around us? What are the ideas behind these laws? In lesson 3, we'll explore how blessings are a framework for reminding us to notice the world around us. Lesson 4 will present Torah commandments governing our relationship to nature, including the mitzvah of *bal tashchit*, which is the basis of Jewish prohibitions against the unnecessary destruction of resources. Lesson 5 deals with Shabbat and *sh'mitah,* the Sabbatical year, *mitzvot* that remind us to take a break from using the world's resources by imposing a regular day (or year) of rest.

Ask students what laws and customs they think should govern our relationship to nature. Invite them to write their thoughts in the journal, page 14.

Lesson 3 — *B'rachot:* Receiving Nature's Gifts

Central Questions: What can the mitzvah of reciting *b'rachot* (blessings) teach us about our relationship to the world around us? How can the different blessings help attune us to nature's bounty and splendor?

Goals: Students will…

1. Recognize the concept of *birchot hanehenin* (blessings of appreciation) in Jewish tradition.
2. Explain how the mitzvah of *b'rachot* (blessings) can teach about our place in the world and our relationship to it.

Introduction

Jewish tradition teaches us to say a *b'rachah*, or blessing, when we enjoy any material pleasure or natural phenomenon. This practice teaches us to stop and thank God for the things we enjoy or consume in this world. It prompts us to reflect on the world and its many wonders and not take them for granted. It encourages us to see ourselves as recipients of the world's bounty and not its owner.

In this lesson we will study various blessings as well as the Talmudic text that discusses why we are commanded to recite blessings.

Materials Needed

Poster board (optional), large sheet of newsprint or butcher paper, marker

Activities

1. Getting Started: What Is a B'rachah? (10 minutes)

Have students do the activity in the journal on page 15 individually or in pairs. *(Answers might include prayer, thank-you, gift, good wishes, grace, ritual.)* Collect the different answers and write them on the board or on a poster-sized copy of the diagram. Try to agree on a definition with the class and write it down. *(For example, a b'rachah is a prayer expressing thanks to God for a particular gift.)*

2. The B'rachah as Reminder (10 minutes)

The Talmud discusses an apparent contradiction between the following two verses in Psalms, regarding who owns the earth, God or humanity.

> To God belongs the earth and everything in it. (Psalms 24:1)
> The heavens, the heavens belong to God, and the earth God gave to humankind. (Psalms 115:16)

Read the verses and ask students to identify the contradiction. Explain that in the Talmud, Rabbi Levi offers this explanation for the contradiction:

> The first verse refers to the state of things before one recites a blessing, and the second refers to the state of things after one has recited a blessing. (Babylonian Talmud, *B'rachot* 35)

Ask students to discuss the purpose of a blessing in pairs or as a class. (*According to Rabbi Levi, a b'rachah is like saying: "God, I recognize that this creation is Yours, and I really appreciate Your letting me enjoy it!"*) If we say and/or think a blessing many times every day, do you think we might adopt a more humble attitude towards nature's (God's) gifts?

You might want to introduce another statement from the same Talmudic discussion:

> Rav Chanina ben Pappa said: Anyone who derives benefit from this world without first reciting a blessing is as if he robs from God.

3. Me and My B'rachot (20 minutes)

This activity is intended to give the students a sense of the rich variety of blessings and how they connect with our senses and our experiences. You can have the students complete the activity in the journal (page 16) individually or in pairs. Alternatively, or as a summation, you might try this:

Ask one of the students to lie down on a large sheet of paper, and trace his or her shape with a thick marker so you have a life-sized human form. Make sure there is room to write around the sides.

Now review the list of blessings and experiences and have students annotate the image, writing each blessing and experience with an arrow connecting it to the appropriate body part. If the students know other blessings, add them, too.

Discuss:

- Talk about the experiences listed, and students' memories and feelings about them. Do we sometimes take the wonders of the world for granted, not really paying attention?
- Point out that many Jews are careful, even today, to recite a blessing for each of these actions and occasions, as a reminder not to take them for granted. Ask: How do you feel about this idea? Do you know anyone who does this?
- Ask whether it's easier to remember to say a *b'rachah* at a "wow" moment, like when we see a rainbow or reach a special occasion (bar/bat mitzvah), or when we do it as a habit, for the everyday "miracles" of having food to eat or clean water to drink.
- Ask students what saying blessings and other expressions of gratitude can teach us about our place in the world. (*It teaches us to be thankful for everything we experience in the world; it prompts us to stop and notice and reflect on the wonders of the world and not take them for granted; it encourages us to see ourselves as recipients of the world's bounty and not its owners.*)

Ask students to try to remember for a whole week to bless a particular experience each time they do it (eating, drinking, etc.). Have the students report on their experience at the next class.

Here are the answers to the exercise on page 16 of the journal:

A. When you see lightning or high mountains or great rivers or any unusual natural phenomena

B. When you see fruit trees flowering in the spring

C. When you eat bread

D. When you drink water or soft drinks

E. When you hear thunder

F. When you smell pleasant spices, plants, or flowers

G. When you put on new clothes

__F.__ *Praised are You, Adonai our God, Ruler of the world, who creates all types of perfumes.*

__B.__ *Praised are You, Adonai our God, Ruler of the world, who didn't leave anything out of God's world and created good things and good trees so people may enjoy them.*

__G.__ *Praised are You, Adonai our God, Ruler of the world, who has given us life, sustained us, and enabled us to reach this time.*

__C.__ *Praised are You, Adonai our God, Ruler of the world, who brings forth bread from the earth.*

__E.__ *Praised are You, Adonai our God, Ruler of the world, whose strength and power fill the world.*

__A.__ *Praised are You, Adonai our God, Ruler of the world, who does acts of creation.*

__D.__ *Praised are You, Adonai our God, Ruler of the world, that all was created by God's word.*

4. Compose a Blessing (10 minutes)

Prompt students to think of a situation they have experienced in nature when it would have felt good to say a blessing of appreciation for the wonderful world we have been given. If possible, take the class outdoors for this activity. Ask students to draw the experience, find a photograph of it, or describe it in words, and then compose a blessing for it in the journal, page 17. Students can finish this activity at home if they need more time. You can make a display, or a booklet, or a web page of these creations.

Further Resources

Visit www.behrmanhouse.com/universe for more resources about b'rachot and the beauty of nature.

Lesson 4 — *Bal Tashchit* (Do Not Destroy)

Central Questions: What do the Torah's laws teach us about our relationship to nature's resources? How can we develop criteria for judging when harm to the environment is justified? What does it mean to "own" land?

Goals: Students will…

1. Be able to explain the concept of *bal tashchit.*
2. Discuss the consequences to the environment of our consumption.

Introduction

The Torah provides important guidelines for our relationship with nature, not only through stories, but also through practical laws. One important example is the principle of *bal tashchit* (from Deuteronomy 20:19-20), which forbids wanton destruction of materials, plants, and man-made products, and has far-ranging environmental implications. While it acknowledges that there are circumstances in which it is unavoidable to be destructive, it admonishes us to be careful of the imprint we leave on the world. This lays a heavy responsibility on each of us, not only to weigh the costs of our actions against their benefits, but also to learn how our actions affect the world.

In this lesson, we will study a few texts that lay out the bare bones of the *bal tashchit* principle and then show how the consumption of the simplest item has far-ranging consequences.

Materials Needed

Bibles or copies of Deuteronomy 20:19-20, magazines

Activities

1. Getting Started: Everyday Impact (20 minutes)

Distribute magazines to the students, or let them go online, and give them 5 minutes to find a picture of someone harming the environment. Ask each student in turn to show their picture to the class, while the other students try to explain what is destructive in the picture.

Now ask the students to draw a picture in the box in the journal (page 18) or find a picture of someone engaged in an activity that is *not* obviously destructive to the environment.

Divide the students into teams of two to three students. Assign each team one of the impact statements from the checklist in the journal (several teams may choose the same statement). Show the pictures of nondestructive activity; ask the teams to examine them in terms of the impact statement they have been assigned and point out environmentally harmful aspects that have been overlooked.

For example, when looking at a picture of a car driving down a road, teams could propose the following:

- Car emissions pollute the air.
- Cars are noisy thus causing noise pollution.
- Cars need roads, which cover land with asphalt.
- The manufacture of cars requires mining of metals, which causes pollution.
- Cars use up petroleum, a fossil fuel (fuel that was produced by nature and can never be renewed or restored).
- Foreign cars used in North America have been transported thousands of miles on ships that use up fossil fuels and pollute the air.

Continue this exercise until it becomes clear that most modern human activity is related to some environmental damage. But since it's not an option to go into hibernation or return to the days of the cavemen, we are left with the constant and inescapable challenge of evaluating every activity and making the best decisions we can as to what environmental damage can be avoided and what is acceptable for the sake of a greater good.

2. Bal Tashchit (10 minutes)

Ask students to complete page 19 in the journal, using the Bible to look up the biblical passage Deuteronomy 20:19-20. Then discuss their findings.

Answers:

The Torah says that you may destroy trees that **do not bear fruit**,
but you may not destroy **fruit** trees.

The Torah explicitly forbids cutting down fruit trees, even during the extreme circumstances of war. In the journal, page 19, we see how Maimonides extends this from trees in wartime to artifacts that are beneficial to the human race, such as dishes, clothes, buildings, and food, at all times. While the Torah forbids the destruction of fruit trees, it does permit the destruction of trees that do not bear fruit. This raises an interesting dilemma: It seems that different parts of nature have different value: we can cut down shade trees to defend ourselves in a war, but not fruit trees. How do we decide when destruction of a resource is justified? Here are some examples of the destruction of items from Maimonides's list that may be justified:

Trees: cutting down trees to make a fire lane in the forest, to prevent the spread of fire; or cutting down trees that have grown too close to a highway and block visibility

Buildings: destruction of buildings that have become dangerously unstable, beyond repair

Ask students to come up with examples of dilemmas where destruction of an item might be acceptable for one purpose but not for another. Here are some examples:

- Using up fossil fuel (a nonrenewable resource) to drive an ambulance versus using fuel to drive an ATV for fun
- Using up petroleum to make plastic for disposable sterile medical equipment versus using plastic for disposable cups and plates

3. What's Your *Bal Tashchit* Score? (15 minutes)

Ask students to take the quiz in their journal (pages 20-21) to see how they impact the environment. Suggest that students add more questions and quiz each other, then take it home and quiz their friends and family.

Enrichment Options

PROJECT BASED LEARNING: ENVIRONMENTAL IMPACT STATEMENT Ask students to choose a product that they use every day (it could be shoes, the chocolate milk they drink at breakfast, their desk, etc.) and try to investigate how the environment was affected in the process of its production. What materials is it made of? Where did the materials come from? How were they transported to the place where the product was made?

Have students prepare an "environmental impact statement" for the particular product they have chosen; this could be a poster or slide show or written report, compiling all the "costs" to the environment, in terms of the different resources used up and collateral damage. The statement could also include suggestions for applying *bal tashchit,* explaining how we, the consumers, could reduce these costs by our purchasing and consumption choices. A collection of these statements could be published as a booklet or on the web, for distribution to the class or beyond.

Using student-driven goals and a real-life presentation, craft a project based learning activity around this topic. See page 64 for more information on project based learning, and also visit www.behrmanhouse.com/project-based-learning.

KNOWLEDGE IS POWER Read the following discussion of Talmud to the students:

> In the Talmud, Mar Zutra said: He who covers an oil lamp or uncovers a kerosene lamp, thus making them burn faster, is sinning against *bal tashchit.*
>
> The warning of *bal tashchit* penetrates all ways of life, teaching us the wisdom of frugality and encouraging us to examine it in all its practical details. If a person is too lazy to look at the details he will surely fail.
>
> (Paraphrased from Rabbi Abraham Isaac Kook, *Ein Aya*, Shabbat 2, chapter 6, 113)

Rabbi Kook quotes an example from the Talmud in which Mar Zutra explains that making a lamp burn faster is sinning against *bal tashchit,* as it is wasteful. Ask students what we can learn from the fact that Mar Zutra talks about two kinds of lamps. *(As Mar Zutra points out, different lamps behave differently, so if we want to avoid waste, we need to know what kind of behavior causes waste. Rabbi Kook points out that if we are lazy and neglect to explore how our behavior affects the environment, we will inevitably sin against* bal tashchit. *We need to continually learn more and examine how our activity affects the environment.)*

Lesson 5 — Taking a Break: Shabbat and *Sh'mitah*

Central Question: How do Shabbat and *sh'mitah,* the Sabbatical year, call on us to honor and redefine our relationship to nature?

Goals: Students will...

1. Articulate the environmental implications of Shabbat and the Sabbatical year (*sh'mitah*).
2. Define *sh'mitah* and discuss the concept that land cannot be fully possessed by humans, that we are not totally free to do with the land as we please.
3. Describe the mitzvah of *sh'mitah.*

Introduction

The concept of Shabbat, of ceasing productive work for one day out of every seven, is generally seen as one of the central commandments of Judaism, based on God's own actions in creating the world, and included in the Ten Commandments. When we try to explain the reasons for Shabbat rules and traditions, we usually do so in terms of its benefit to humans: providing opportunities for rest, for focus on the spiritual, for being with family, etc. In this lesson, we will take a slightly different perspective, focusing on what we can learn from Shabbat about our place in the universe.

The commandment of *sh'mitah* is a corollary of the weekly Shabbat. This commandment, which applies only to Jews in the Land of Israel, requires that we let the land "rest" every seven years: for a full year, the land is not to be plowed, planted, or harvested (Exodus 23:10-11, Leviticus 25:1-7). Because of its agricultural nature, *sh'mitah* expresses even more strongly than Shabbat the importance of limiting our exploitation of the earth. Both Shabbat and *sh'mitah* have implications for how we live today.

In ancient Israel, Jews lived in an agrarian society. The land was not only the people's ancestral inheritance but their means of livelihood. The Torah contains a number of laws that relate specifically to Jewish agriculture in the land of Israel, including the rules of tithing and gleaning; the agricultural aspects of Pesach, Shavuot, and Sukkot; the Jubilee year (Leviticus 25:8-34); and *sh'mitah.*

The mitzvah of *sh'mitah* can be explained in several ways:

- Theology: The land is not really ours to own. We are not free to use it or profit from it in any way we want. It belongs to God and the use of it is allowed only in accordance with God's rules.
- Social justice: By forbidding cultivation and outlawing private ownership of the crops that come up on their own during the *sh'mitah* year, the commandment helps ease the distance between classes and provides for the poor with dignity.

Activities

1. Getting Started: What Is Not Ours (10 minutes)

Have the students do the exercise in the journal, page 22, individually. Then invite them to share their answers and discuss their thinking. Ask: How should we treat items that do not belong to us? (*We are not free to do what we want with other people's possessions; we should accept the owners' authority to tell us how to behave with respect to their possessions.*) You might invite students to recount real life experiences along the same lines.

Remind students of the question we encountered in lesson 1, about whether humanity's role in the world is to do with it as we wish or to be responsible for its care.

2. Rest and Renewal (15 minutes)

Pair students and have them read the fourth commandment in the journal on page 23. Ask them to come up with reasons for why we are supposed to rest on Shabbat, and how the environment can benefit from our day of rest. Discuss their responses. (*We don't own the world so it's not ours to use without limit; we all need time to rest and be renewed; a day of rest helps us focus on our families or our spiritual lives; a day of rest helps preserve the resources of the world from our tendency to use them up without stopping.*)

Seneca, like other Greek and Roman philosophers, thought that Shabbat was a sign of laziness; he couldn't understand why the Jews didn't just follow the natural human inclination to struggle constantly to control and use the natural world for human benefit. Have students write their responses to Seneca; see if the class can agree on a clear statement of the environmental implications of Shabbat.

3. The Sabbatical Year (20 minutes)

Have students read the text of the Torah about the Sabbatical year (journal, page 24) in pairs, or read it together with them as a full class activity. Have them consider how it would be possible, in reality, to obey this law. A few notes:

- The text refers specifically to the Land of Israel and to the Jews living there, therefore it doesn't affect food grown there by non-Jews or food grown elsewhere. So you could buy food from your non-Jewish neighbors or import it.
- You can't work the land, but you can eat (but not sell) from what grows by itself, including fruit from trees or crops that come up from seeds that dropped naturally the previous year.
- You can take care of your livestock, and eat them and their products (milk, eggs) with no restriction.
- Note that the challenges of the Sabbatical year actually last for more than a year, because you wouldn't have food to harvest immediately after the Sabbatical year ends, since you can't plant during *sh'mitah.*

Discuss: How is *sh'mitah* similar to and different from Shabbat? (*Sh'mitah applies only in Israel, only to specific activities and crops; it is probably much harder to observe since it's a whole year, but its message is the same: this world does not belong to you, and there are limits to your right to exploit it, even if those limits cause you significant inconvenience and even suffering.*)

Discuss: What rules and customs could we modern, nonagricultural people observe that would convey the same message and help remind us not to use up the world's resources without limit? Could some form of *sh'mitah* be relevant and realistic in our setting? (*For example, some professions, like teaching, offer the possibility of a sabbatical year.*)

Enrichment Options

PUZZLE TIME: "SEVENS" CROSSWORD If students have extra time before class or while other students are completing their work, they can work on the "Sevens" crossword puzzle in the journal, page 25.

Answers:

Across	**Down**
2. zayin	1. RoshHashanah
5. Pharaoh	3. Tishre
7. shmitah	4. Shavuot
9. David	6. Pesach
10. week	7. Shabbat
11. rested	8. menorah
12. nothing	

SH'MITAH CONTROVERSY For hundreds of years, until the 1800s, there were almost no Jewish farmers in the land of Israel. But when Jews began returning to the land and began farming it, they had to decide how to relate to the commandment of the Sabbatical year. This led to interesting solutions and an ongoing, bitter debate. Ask students to learn about the Sabbatical year in Israel today and prepare a presentation or poster explaining possible ways of interpreting it, as well as different solutions to the debate. Links to useful articles for exploring different views and events of recent years can be found in the Further Resources section below.

AGRICULTURE IN THE TORAH *Sh'mitah*, with its focus on the connection of the Jewish people to the Land of Israel, is just one example of many laws and customs that emphasize this connection. It is possible to look at all the agricultural laws and holidays of the Torah as reminders of our dependence on nature. Here are a few suggestions for exploring this idea:

- The cycles of the moon are central to the Jewish calendar. Have students, or teams, keep moon diaries for a month or so, making daily notations of the moon's appearance, and times of rising and/or setting. Compare the results to the Jewish calendar for the same period.
- Study with the class the agricultural components of the three festivals, Passover, Shavuot, and Sukkot, examining how they are tied to the seasons in Israel: Leviticus 23, especially verses 4-21 and 33-43.
- Study the laws of gleaning (Leviticus 23:22, for example), as a further way of stating that our ownership of "our" land is limited, and we are not free to exploit it 100 percent for ourselves. Discuss: How could this have a modern interpretation/application?

Further Resources

Visit www.behrmanhouse.com/universe for more background on the Sabbatical year and the controversy surrounding it in Israel today.

CHAPTER

3

The Animal Kingdom

We humans have a special relationship to one part of the universe, the animal kingdom, since we are ourselves animals. Thus our desire to exploit this part of creation often runs up against our feeling of identification with our fellow animals, and leads to ambivalence regarding the morality of our treatment of them. Lesson 6 takes a global view, looking at the value of biodiversity, the variety of life forms. Lesson 7 focuses more on the morality of our treatment of the animals around us, looking at the Jewish perspective on cruelty to animals in general and on our right to eat them.

Invite students to write their thoughts about how we should treat animals on page 26 in their journals.

Lesson 6 — Biodiversity

Central Question: Why is biodiversity important?

Goals: Students will…

1. Discuss the extinction of species and human attitudes towards extinction going back to the story of Noah's Ark.
2. Reflect upon the underlying reasons for maintaining biodiversity.

Introduction

Biodiversity, the variety of all forms of life, has been substantially impacted in North America due to the destruction and fragmentation of animals' natural habitats, particularly as a result of the clearance of trees and underbrush for agriculture, and the impact of massive hunting (as in the case of the American bison) and poisoning campaigns (applied against wolves). Many species have already become extinct, and others are on the way.

Some would say that the disappearance of species is an unavoidable part of the ongoing drama of nature and of our own life as a species; others argue that humans have a special obligation to avoid actions that might cause such extinctions, for several reasons:

- There may be potential benefits to humans from species at risk of extinction, such as not-yet-discovered medicines.
- Extinctions could upset the fragile ecological balance, without which the environment could descend into chaos.
- The biblical Creation story (Genesis chapter 1) includes the recurring refrain: "And God saw that this was good." If everything created is good, then it has intrinsic value—a right to exist, regardless of whether or not it benefits humanity.
- According to the concept of *bal tashchit*, which we studied in lesson 4, we are obligated to respect and preserve the world and are not free to destroy it.

Materials Needed

Bibles, Internet-connected computer and projector (if possible)

Activities

1. Getting Started: Noah's Ark (15 minutes)

Ask the students to read Genesis 6:9-22, then look at Edward Hicks's painting *Noah's Ark* in their journal, page 27, and answer the questions that follow. Ask students to share their answers. The painting shows farm animals and zoo animals, and omits pests such as rats, snakes, skunks, and spiders. This is a natural impulse by the artist, whether or not it was intentional: Why save animals that are seen as a nuisance?

Read the Rabbi Karo quote together and ask students if they think the world would be a better place without some animals.

2. King David and the Spider (15 minutes)

Ask the students to read the story about King David on page 28, and then ask for volunteers (playing the narrator, David, God, King Saul, and the spider in the cave) to act it out.

After the story has been acted out, discuss David's realization that all creations are potentially useful to us, even if we don't understand how. Ask the students to think of examples. *(Possible answers include medicines made from rare rainforest plants, which could not have been discovered if the plants had become extinct; insects that serve a key role in pollinating flowers to produce the fruit we eat; and krill, tiny shrimp near the bottom of the marine food chain that serve a key role in the ecological balance—if they became extinct, most marine life, including the fish we eat, would follow suit.)*

Explain that, at God's command, Noah used his ark to save all the animals from wholesale extinction. Nowadays, many plants and animals are threatened with extinction by the actions of humankind, from deliberate eradication of some species to destruction of habitat. Some of these extinctions have unexpected consequences, a domino effect that threatens to destroy the ecological equilibrium.

Ask students to read the definition of biodiversity on page 28, and give examples of an environment with high biodiversity and one with low biodiversity. (*Tropical rainforests have the highest degree of biodiversity, with more than half of the world's plant and animal species, including many different kinds of land animals, birds, insects, fish, trees, shrubs, small plants, moss, etc. Deserts have low biodiversity, with very limited plant and animal life.*)

3. The Case of the Spotted Owl (20 minutes)

Ask students to read the story of the spotted owl controversy, page 29 in the journal.

Encourage students to search online for more information. They can follow the links found on www.behrmanhouse.com/universe.

Divide the class into teams, each representing one of the following groups:

- Environmentalists
- Logging company executives
- Logging company employees
- Hikers in Pacific Northwest forests
- Residents near Pacific Northwest forests

Facilitate a debate on the question, "Should logging be banned in the forests of the Pacific Northwest to protect the spotted owl from extinction?" Each team should represent their group in the debate. Here are some arguments that may be mentioned:

- *Many jobs could be lost if logging is banned. People depend on those jobs to support their families.*
- *Owls thrive in our many national parks, so maybe they will be able to survive in reduced forests, even with logging activity around them.*
- *Maybe some future scientist will discover that a lifesaving medicine can be extracted from the owls. If they become extinct, we may never know what we've lost.*

- *Spotted owls control the population of mice; if the owls disappear, the mouse population will grow and expand beyond the forest, damaging crops.*
- *The commandment of* bal tashchit *indicates that we have no right to destroy a species.*
- *Humans are responsible to take care of God's creation.*

As students debate, consider suggesting the idea of finding a middle ground, such as introducing restrictions on logging rather than an outright ban.

To wrap up the lesson, ask students to try to imagine what the world would be like without some of its creatures. Do we have the right to destroy a species?

Enrichment Options

PROJECT BASED LEARNING: PREVENTING EXTINCTION Ask students to find out what native animals or plants are under threat of extinction in your area and why this is so. What needs to be changed to help prevent extinction? Encourage students to see if there's anything they can do, either by joining a campaign targeted at the problem, changing their behavior, or convincing others to change (for example, by writing a letter to a company that is polluting).

Doing this research will help students see that the issues they're studying in class are literally "close to home." This project helps them transition from theoretical knowledge to personal action. Encourage students to report any successes (or even instructive failures) they have with this project.

Using student-driven goals and a real-life presentation, craft a project based learning activity around this topic. See page 64 for more information on project based learning, and also visit www.behrmanhouse.com/project-based-learning.

Further Resources

Visit www.behrmanhouse.com/universe for more resources about biodiversity, about the spotted owl controversy in the Pacific Northwest, and about species threatened by extinction.

Lesson 7 — *Tza'ar Ba'alei Chayim* (Kindness to Animals)

Central Questions: How should human beings relate to and treat animals? Do human needs have priority over animal needs?

Goals: Students will…

1. Explain the Torah teaching of *tza'ar ba'alei chayim* (the mitzvah of showing kindness to animals).
2. Talk about practical lessons we can deduce from Jewish laws and practices regarding animals, including Jewish attitudes toward eating meat.
3. Discuss the conflicts that can arise between the needs of humans and of animals.

Introduction

Animals are living creatures. They possess physical and emotional needs and experience pain and suffering. However human beings have the ability to use animals for work, food, and other purposes.

Jewish thought is considerate of all living creatures. There are concrete Jewish laws that indicate the obligation to care for animals and mitigate their suffering, as well as a prohibition against causing suffering. This principle is known as *tza'ar ba'alei chayim*, which translates literally as "the suffering of living creatures."

At the same time Judaism recognizes and justifies humanity's need to use animals for its own benefit. There is a certain tension between these two principles. If we are commanded not to hurt animals, how can we kill them or use them as beasts of burden? One answer is that killing an animal for food or some other need is not considered a violation of *tza'ar ba'alei chayim,* since humanity's essential needs are given priority. Each case needs to be carefully examined and decided after weighing humanity's need and benefit against the extent of the animals' discomfort and suffering.

In the previous lessons we saw that there are different ways of viewing humanity's place in Creation. This question arises even more acutely regarding animals. Are we all equal inhabitants of the planet and therefore all have equal rights to exist and be left alone? Or do humans enjoy a privileged status that justifies using animals for our own needs, be it labor, transportation, or food? Are all living creatures to be treated equally, or is there a difference between how we must treat domesticated animals and wild ones? Cockroaches and cows? Ants and elephants?

This lesson is intended to make the students aware of this tension and the questions that come with it. We will examine the Jewish sources that govern the relationship between humans and animals in general terms. One of the issues that brings these two principles into direct conflict is the question of killing animals as a food source. We will examine this question in the context of raising students' consciousness about a wide variety of environmental/ethical concerns. Please note that the goal is *not* to advocate for any one specific lifestyle change.

Materials Needed

Toy stuffed cat, Bibles (for optional enrichment activity), materials for project (if being done as a class): newspapers and magazines, scissors, scrapbook, glue

Activities

1. Getting Started: Animals and Us (5 minutes)

Brainstorm with students a list of ways we interact with animals. Alternatively, students can write their responses in the journal, page 30. *(Possible answers:* **Wildlife:** *observing in nature, damaging or protecting their habitats, hunting for food or for sport, being hunted (e.g., by bears, mosquitoes), competing for resources (e.g., with ants, mice).* **Farm animals:** *raising for food, eating eggs or milk, using their skins or fur, farm work.* **Pets:** *taking care of them, playing with them.* **Other:** *horse racing and other sports, guide dogs, police dogs, scientific testing of medicines or cosmetics.)*

Introduce the idea that Jewish law, and specifically the mitzvah *tza'ar ba'alei chayim*, can help guide us in thinking about the relationship between humans and animals.

2. Taking Care of Animals: A Simulation (15 minutes)

Tell the class that we're going to examine the conflicts that can arise between the needs of humans and of animals. Ask them to imagine that they have decided to adopt a class cat. (If possible, bring a toy stuffed cat to class as a prop to generate excitement.) Give students five minutes on their own to list the needs of the cat and the needs of the students in the class (journal, page 30), making it clear that this is just an exercise not an actual decision. (*For example, the cat needs food and water every day, room to play and roam, attention, a place to sharpen its claws, a litter box. Students need money to buy cat food, someone to feed the cat when they're not there, the ability to focus on classwork when they are, a classroom that doesn't smell like a litter box.*)

Together as a class or in small groups the students must decide how to take care of the cat. To do so they will need to address the following questions and draw up a list of instructions and rules.

- What will we do with the cat after school hours and on school holidays? (*For example, let it roam free in the synagogue building, take turns bringing it home, ask other members of the synagogue to take turns taking care of it.)*
- What are we going to feed the cat? *(For example, give the cat some of our own food, let the cat fend for itself by hunting mice or scavenging from the garbage, or chip in to buy cat food.)*
- What will we do if the cat scratches or bites someone in the class? How will we prevent that from happening again? How will that affect the cat? (*confine it to a cage, trim its claws, have it declawed by a veterinarian)*
- What will we do if the cat has kittens? (*raise all the cats, give the kittens away*)
- What are the benefits to having a class cat? (*It's cute; perhaps we can learn from observing it—such as how far it can jump, or what its body language tells us; we can use the cat to get rid of mice.)*

List the decisions and rules on the board. Be sure to steer the discussion to concrete answers and plans, pointing out the pros and cons of each option as to how it benefits or harms the students *and* how it benefits or harms the cat. By the end, the students should be aware of the difficulty in satisfying both their needs and those of the cat.

3. What the Torah Tells Us: Humans and Animals (10 minutes)

Divide the class into small groups and have each group work together to match the Torah and Talmud texts in their journals (page 31) to the lessons we can learn from this text. There may be multiple answers for each text and for each lesson. Here are suggested responses:

Texts	Lessons
1. If you see the donkey of someone who hates you fallen under its load, you must not ignore him, but be sure to help him with it. (Exodus 23:5) **A, D, F** 2. A person cannot sit down to eat until he has fed his animals. (Babylonian Talmud *B'rachot* 40A) **B, D** 3. If you happen to notice a bird's nest along the road, whether in a tree or on the ground, and there are chicks or eggs with the mother bird sitting on them, you must not take the mother with the young. You must be sure to let the mother go, but you may take the young for yourself. (Deuteronomy 22:6-7) **E, F, G** 4. You must not muzzle your ox when it is threshing grain. (Deuteronomy 25:4) **C, E, F, G** 5. When an ox, lamb, or goat is born, it must be under the care of its mother seven days, but from the eighth day onward it will be acceptable as an offering gift to the Lord. You must not slaughter an ox or a sheep and its young on the same day. (Leviticus 22:27-28) **E, F, G**	**A.** *Don't stand by when you see animals suffering.* **B.** *Take care of your animals before you take care of yourself.* **C.** *Appreciate and repay the help animals give you by helping them.* **D.** *You are responsible to take care of your animal's needs.* **E.** *Don't upset animals unnecessarily.* **F.** *Treat animals compassionately.* **G.** *We can use animals for our own needs.*

Ask each group to choose one rule and discuss whether the rule is for the animal's benefit or for human beings' benefit, then rewrite the rule for modern times. Share with the class. (*For example, you could rewrite #1 as follows: If you see a stray dog hanging around the neighborhood, you must take care of it and find it a home or at least a shelter.*)

As a conclusion remind them that the term *tza'ar ba'alei chayim* translates as "the suffering of living creatures." Jewish law allows human beings to use animals for their own needs but not to cause them to suffer. This principle must be considered whenever we use or care for animals.

4. Should We Eat Animals? (10 minutes)

In the Bible, right after the Creation of the world, God tells Adam and Eve what they are supposed to eat. (Genesis 1:29-30) After the Flood, God instructs Noah about what he may eat. (Genesis 9:3-4) Ask students, either individually or as a class, to turn to page 32 in the journal and then read and compare the verses and write in the foods that are allowed in the spaces provided.

(Answers: Instructions to Adam and Eve—they can eat plants, which includes fruits and vegetables. They can't eat animals such as mammals, fish, birds, bugs, etc. Instructions to Noah—humans can eat plants and animals. They can't eat animals that are still alive or blood.)

Discuss: Why do you think the rules changed?
(Possible answers: Tell students that Jewish thinkers throughout the ages have asked the same question [why did the rules change?] and come up with different answers. These include: people were eating/killing animals anyway, people needed more food, when people couldn't eat animals they acted cruelly to one another. Maybe if they could eat animals they would realize that they are different from animals and treat each other better; they would learn that they are important and responsible for animals.)

5. **Moderation** (10 minutes)

Ask the class to share what they ate for dinner last night or what their favorite dinner is. Write their answers on the board under the headings:

- Meat
- Vegetarian

Ask the students to indicate in the journal (page 33) how often they eat meat.

Discuss:

- Why do you eat meat? (*it tastes good, nutrition, because my parents serve it to me)*
- If there are any vegetarians in the class ask them why they don't eat meat. (*not healthy, my parents don't serve it, not environmentally friendly, cruel to animals)*

Encourage a discussion about the reasons for or against eating meat.

Ask students to consider the possibility that eating meat doesn't have to be an all-or-nothing decision. Perhaps the way to both respect the sanctity of animal life and accept our own nature as omnivores is to pursue an approach of moderation in eating meat. Read together the passage on moderation in eating meat from Maimonides's code, the *Mishneh Torah* (Laws of Opinions 5:10). Ask students to discuss the range of options for finding an appropriate balance between human needs and the needs of other creatures.

Enrichment Options

PUZZLE TIME: BIBLICAL ANIMALS If students have extra time before class or while other students are completing their work, they can work on the biblical animal crossword puzzle in the journal, page 34.

Answers:

Across
5. lion
6. ostrich
8. eagle
10. wolf
12. raven
13. horses

Down
1. foxes
2. dove
3. stork
4. fish
7. hawk
9. goats
11. fawns

BIBLICAL DRAMA Read together the story of Balaam and his disobedient donkey (Numbers 22:21-33). This is an example of biblical humor, in which the prophet Balaam is less able to see the angel of God than is his donkey. Balaam gets angrier and angrier, beating the poor donkey repeatedly. Students might enjoy dramatizing or illustrating this story, which raises the question of whether sometimes animals may be more "human" than people are.

HELPING ANIMALS Challenge students to think about ways they can help animals, such as by volunteering at a local animal shelter, adopting a stray, or buying food that is raised or manufactured humanely, like eggs from free-range chickens. Focus on practical projects for individuals or the class as a whole. It might be interesting to invite a guest speaker who is involved in animal rights issues on some level (medical researcher, dog shelter worker, animal rights activist).

ANIMAL WATCH SCRAPBOOK Make an Animal Watch scrapbook, with articles and/or pictures from newspapers, magazines, or the Internet, that depicts the different ways humans treat and/or use animals. One section can have all positive interactions between animals and people, and the other side can be about negative or more complicated ones. Try to come to some conclusions about the relationship between humans and animals based on the scrapbook. This could also be a class bulletin board.

VEGETARIAN CLASS COOKBOOK Make a vegetarian cookbook, individually or as a class project. Collect meat-free recipes from family, friends, and/or the Internet, and print them together in a cookbook.

Further Resources

Visit www.behrmanhouse.com/universe for more information about animal rights versus human rights, *sh'chitah* (kosher slaughtering of animals), vegetarianism, and ecology.

CHAPTER

4

Sharing Public Resources

One of the key concepts in discussions of environmental ethics is the "public space," the resources that belong to no one, and therefore belong to everyone. The questions of who is responsible for common resources and who may set limits on their exploitation are central in public discourse on a wide range of issues. The concept of public versus private space and the individual's responsibility for "the commons" is dealt with extensively in the Talmud and later sources, and is explored in lesson 8. Then lesson 9 deals with a specific application of the concept, in the area of water conservation.

As an introduction to this chapter, invite students to journal their thoughts about the sharing of natural resources on page 36 of the journal.

Lesson 8 — The Commons

Central Question: How can we balance the individual's self-interest and the public good?

Goals: Students will…

1. Explain the concept of "the commons," our shared resources, or *r'shut harabim.*

2. Recognize the dilemmas this entails and the responsibility it lays upon us.

Introduction

Elements of our environment are often referred to as "the commons"; this includes resources such as land, air, and water that are shared, used, and enjoyed by all. In 1968, American scientist Garrett Hardin published an influential article titled "The Tragedy of the Commons." The term "commons" refers to any shared resource; the "tragedy" is that if each person sharing the resource acts in his/her own apparent rational self-interest, in the end the resource will be used up, and everyone will suffer.

Examples of such occurrences abound: The owners of factories that pollute the air and water profit by avoiding the cost of purifiers, but in the long run are poisoning their workforce. Farmers that overgraze public land earn more profits by grazing more cattle, but they are severely depleting the land so in the long run it may not be able to sustain any cattle. All of us tend to use our cars as if there were an infinite supply of gasoline in the world, but in fact we know that one day the supply will run out.

It is clear that short-term approaches are often unsustainable in the long run, and people need to understand and act upon their joint responsibility for environmental resources.

Materials Needed

Dishes (one for each group of four students), one pair of chopsticks for each student, jellybeans

Activities

1. Getting Started: Our Shared Resources (5 minutes)

Brainstorm with students a list of natural resources that are shared, used, and enjoyed by all. Write the list on the board. (*air, oceans, sources of fresh water, oil, green space, the sun*) Explain that these shared resources are often referred to as "the commons," because they belong to everyone in common, but not to anyone in particular.

2. The Commons Fishing Game (25 minutes)

Adapted from the lesson plan "The Tragedy of the Commons," copyright © by Jeremy Szerlip, Scarsdale, NY (www.scienceteacherprogram.org/biology/szerlip03.html)

Divide the class into groups of four students. Seat each group around a table. Put a dish containing 16 jellybeans in the middle of the table, and supply each student with a pair of chopsticks.

Ask students to imagine that the dish is a lake, the jellybeans are fish, and the chopsticks are fishing equipment. Explain the rules: "The fish in the lake are the only food source for your starving family, and your task is to catch them. Every year you get one chance to take as many fish as you can from the lake. Your family needs to eat at least 2 fish a year to avoid starvation. You can keep the rest of the fish you catch, which your family can eat in subsequent years or trade to vary their diet. At the end of each year, the remaining fish in the lake will reproduce."

The game proceeds as follows:

- Allot 1 minute for every "year" of the game. During that time, students decide how many fish to take for that year.
- Tell students that the game must proceed in silence; there is to be no communication between players.
- At the end of each "year," double the number of fish that remain in each lake, as the fish reproduce. Check on the supplies of each player: the families of players that have less than two fish starve, so those players are out of the game. The remaining players fill in the data in the chart on page 37.
- After the jellybeans for this year have been eaten, proceed to the next "year."
- Run the game for 5 "years" and ask students to fill in the data table in their journals after each "year."

After the game has run its course and students have had a few minutes to summarize in their journals, compare notes among the groups, and discuss the following questions:

- Did you take more fish than you needed? Why or why not? What about the other members of your group?
- Now that you've seen the course of the game, would you have played it differently?

Explain that this game is used to illustrate the difficulty of managing shared resources in real life. For example, over the past 50 years, because of the high demand for fish, commercial fishermen have adopted more efficient and aggressive methods to catch more fish. But in many places they have put themselves out of business, as fish populations have dried up. This has happened with codfish in the North Sea, and bluefin tuna in the Mediterranean Sea.

Discuss: Using what you have learned from the course of the game, can you advise people how to use shared resources wisely? Suggest that students imagine a conversation between a poor fisherman who needs to support his family now and a fisherman who wants his son to inherit his business and support his family 20 years from now. How can such conflicts be resolved? Through education? Laws?

3. **Stone Pollution** (15 minutes)

Read (or retell in your own words) the story from the Talmud found in the journal, page 38. Discuss: What did the wise man mean when he said that the commons—in this case, the road—belongs to the farmer?

Ask students, individually or in small groups, to write and illustrate a brief story using the comic book panels in their journals. Their story should demonstrate the idea of the commons using examples that are more related to their lives. Examples could include people throwing garbage into the street, factories polluting the air or water, etc.

End the lesson by reminding students of some insights from the game, such as how tempting it is to overuse common resources and how we all eventually pay the price.

Enrichment Options

NEW RULES FOR FISHING Ask students to experiment with the fishing game they played in class and try to propose a new rule that players can follow so they can obtain the maximum number of fish while still sustaining populations in the lake. Students should explain the advantages of their proposed rule: How fair is it? How simple is it to follow?

Several different rules can be proposed, each with its pros and cons. Students may need to decide if a rule should be the same for all—that is, should all families be allowed the same number of fish—or if it should be adjustable (for example, poor families might be allowed more fish to help them survive). Should the rule be simple, stating one number as the maximum, or should it be more dynamic, taking into account the current number of fish in the lake and adjusting accordingly? Ask: Would a rule or rules like this help in the real world? Why or why not?

Further Resources

Visit www.behrmanhouse.com/universe for a link to the original "Tragedy of the Commons" fishing game.

Lesson 9 — Using Water Wisely

Central Questions: What is the nature of our obligation to conserve scarce resources like water? What are the limits of that obligation?

Goals: Students will…

1. Be aware of the importance of rain and water in Talmudic sources as well as in our lives today.
2. Be conscious of the need for water conservation as well as the questions it raises globally and in North America.

Introduction

Water is the basis of all life, essential for drinking, agriculture, washing, etc. As the world population grows, fresh water (as opposed to sea water, which is salty) is becoming an increasingly precious resource. Different parts of the world, including parts of North America, have faced decreased rainfalls over the last decade. At the same time, the demand for water has increased due to rising populations and growing industry. Worldwide demand for fresh water tripled during the last century and is now doubling every 21 years. At the same time more and more water sources are suffering from pollution and contamination. United Nations analysis suggests that the world will face a 40 percent global shortfall between demand and supply of fresh water by the year 2030. Because of the interlinked global economy, this growing stress on the world's water will affect food and energy systems all around the world.

Globally there is a growing awareness of the need to manage and conserve water on both individual and national levels. This awareness of the precariousness of man's dependence on water is not new, and we find several stories and sources in the Bible and rabbinic literature that illustrate man's dependence on rain and water. In this lesson we will examine a source in the Torah that emphasizes man's dependence on rain, and we will study a traditional prayer for rain found in the siddur. We will compare the need for water then and now, and the ways in which we can conserve water today.

Materials Needed

Poster of a house or floor plans, with room to write on; poster board; markers; printouts of Water Conservation Ideas handout, from www.behrmanhouse.com/universe.

Advance preparation: Draw a simple house diagram on the poster board. Label the kitchen, bathroom, yard, and laundry room.

Activities

1. Getting Started: We Need Water For… (5 minutes)

Brainstorm with students about the different ways in which they or their families use water. Write the answers on the board. Have the class try to organize the list in order of importance, and discuss the various ways we use water. Alternatively, have the class imagine what they would do if their water supply were turned off for a day, for a week, or indefinitely.

2. Why Do We Need Rain? (10 minutes)

Have the students, either individually or in pairs, read Deuteronomy 11:10-12, about the importance of rain in Israel, then fill in the blanks in the journal, page 39. Discuss together the advantages and disadvantages of the water supply in Egypt compared to that in the Land of Israel.

Answers:

In Egypt, the **farmers** provided water for their **fields** from the Nile River, through their own hard work. But the land in Israel gets its water from **rain**. Farmers there are **dependent** on nature and God to provide water. This should teach us that water is **limited** and precious, and we should use it **sparingly**.

Given the land of Israel's need for rain, ask the students to imagine what would happen if it didn't rain. How would that affect the people? What could they do if it didn't rain?

Explain that rain (or lack of it) plays a major role in a number of biblical episodes. Famine caused by drought was a familiar disaster scenario: For example, Abraham's wandering to Egypt (Genesis 12:10), or Joseph's brothers coming down to Egypt (Genesis 42:1-5). In fact, an entire tractate of the Talmud, *Ta'anit*, deals with the instructions for praying and fasting when there is a rain shortage in Israel. The assumption was that a drought was brought about by God's anger for our sins.

3. In Search of Fresh Water (10 minutes)

Have students read the paragraph on page 40 in the journal and discuss the possible responses to freshwater shortages today. Discuss their ideas for other solutions, with special emphasis on the question of what each of us can actually do about the problem. This will bring us to the option—and obligation—of conservation, which we will focus on in the next activity. Visit www.behrmanhouse.com/universe for links to information on innovative freshwater technologies.

4. How Can I Conserve Water? (15 minutes)

Give the class a few minutes to fill in their suggestions for how to conserve water (journal, page 41). Then, using a poster board showing a simple house diagram, write down their suggestions for how to save water in the kitchen, bathroom, yard, and laundry room.

If possible you can let the class look up information or play online games to give them ideas. You can find links at www.behrmanhouse.com/universe.

If the class needs help coming up with ideas, you can prompt them with questions, such as:

- What uses more water, a bath or shower?
- Are there times when we let the water run even when no one is really using it?
- Do you check to see if your jeans are really dirty before you throw them in the wash?
- When is the best time to water the grass?

For a handout with a list of water conservation ideas, visit: www.behrmanhouse.com/universe.

5. Prayer for Rain (10 minutes)

Like Native Americans and other indigenous peoples, our ancestors prayed for rain. Discuss the reasons people prayed for rain. (*For example, they believed droughts were a punishment from God; public prayers helped motivate the people to improve their behavior; prayer gave people hope and expressed their faith that in the end, God would take care of them.*) Read the prayer for rain (journal, page 42) responsively with the class. You can appoint one or two students to lead the prayer and have the rest respond with the parts in italics.

Discuss: Why does the prayer mention examples of people who experienced God's miracles regarding water? (*to give the people hope; to remind God that God provided our people with miracles throughout the ages*)

Note that this prayer is not meant for a time of drought but is said every year on Shemini Atzeret. Ask: What does this tell us about the people's hopes and fears as they looked forward to the rainy season, which was approaching? (*Since it rains only between October and April in Israel, they were in great need of rain by the time Sukkot came in September or October; they looked forward anxiously to the rainy season, since a dry winter would be a disaster.*)

Have the students compose their own prayer for rain and water conservation, reflecting some of what was discussed in class, on page 43. When would they recommend saying the prayer? Invite some of the students to read their prayers aloud. The class can put together a water prayer book.

In preparation for the next lesson (Lesson 10), assign students to fill out the Waste Inventory chart in the journal, page 45, for three days. You can also print copies of this chart from www.behrmanhouse.com/universe.

Enrichment Options

WATER CONSERVATION PROJECTS Ask students what they can do to encourage water conservation. For example, they might want to make a poster with conservation ideas and hang it up where everyone can see. They can then decide or vote on one or two things to implement in their class or school, such as setting up a rain barrel to save rainfall and using the water to water the plants in and around school, putting flow restrictors on taps, channeling the drains from the drinking fountains into the garden, or putting up water conservation posters over sinks.

PROJECT BASED LEARNING: CONSERVING NATURAL RESOURCES Water is just one example of a vital yet scarce resource. In the experience of people in the Land of Israel, it is *the* vital yet scarce resource. However, the same challenge faces us today with respect to other resources, such as fossil fuels (which we will explore further in lesson 11), clean air, and even fish (as we saw in lesson 8). Ask students to translate the ideas and suggestions we discussed regarding water to the problem of other natural resources. They can research the scale of the problem, bring suggestions for solutions, and propose conservation projects. They might also want to explore a moral dilemma: If we are confident that a technological solution will be found, are we free of the obligation to conserve?

Using student-driven goals and a real-life presentation, craft a project based learning activity around this topic. See page 64 for more information on project based learning, and also visit www.behrmanhouse.com/project-based-learning.

Further Resources

Visit www.behrmanhouse.com/universe for more resources on water conservation and freshwater projects, plus hints on how to save water in the home.

CHAPTER

5

Our Responsibility to the Future

A central concept in discussing environmental ethics is the responsibility to future generations. What is our obligation to the future? What can we be expected to change for the well-being of those who come after us? Lesson 10 deals with the question of what we "need" versus what we "want." How small of a footprint are we obligated to make? Must we lower our own standard of living for the sake of those who will live in the future? Might living more simply and modestly actually improve our way of life, right now? In our time, perhaps no issue raises this question more acutely than the phenomenon of climate change caused by human activity. Lesson 11 covers the scientific and ethical aspects of global warming and the imperative for sustainable practices especially with regard to our energy use. Lesson 12 explores how we can approach the daunting challenges that climate change presents us with by breaking a large task into small steps.

As an introduction to this chapter, invite students to journal their thoughts about their responsibility to future generations (journal, page 44).

Lesson 10 — How Much Is Too Much?

Central Questions: What is *necessary* consumption? What knowledge, and habits, can help us reduce the amount of resources we use?

Goals: Students will…

1. Discuss the environmental imperative of reducing consumption.
2. Talk about the relationship between material possessions and perceived wealth.
3. Explain the connection between the value of modesty (being satisfied by filling our basic needs) and reducing consumption.

Introduction

In popular discourse on the environment, the focus is usually on recycling and on buying "green" products. These are important ideas. For various reasons, however, one of the key elements of environmental strategy is often lost in the noise: reducing consumption. This simple imperative goes against many messages, conscious and subconscious, that bombard us all the time in Western culture. Hearing it and incorporating it into our consciousness and behavior is a big challenge. Meeting that challenge may be the only way to really change our world. This lesson asks "how much is enough," and "how much is too much." We will look at the cultural forces that drive increased consumption and try to find a balance between satisfying **needs** and indulging **wants**, and discuss the role of advertising in convincing us to buy (consume) more than we thought we needed.

Materials Needed

Internet-connected computer and projector, youth magazines of any type (one for every two students)

Advance preparation: A week before this lesson, assign students to fill out the Waste Inventory chart in the journal, page 45, over three days. You can also print copies of this chart from the website, at www.behrmanhouse.com/universe.

Activities

1. Getting Started: The Waste Inventory (10 minutes)

Ask students to share the results of the Waste Inventory chart (journal, page 45) that they filled out during the previous week.

Discuss the following:

- What were the reasons for discarding edible food? *(they cooked too much, took too much on their plate, bought too much, a restaurant served too much, they disliked the food).*
- Is this a topic of family discussion? Is it a problem?
- What could be done to reduce the waste? (*think twice before filling our plate, convince our parents to cook only foods we like!, suggest to restaurants that they don't serve oversized portions)*

The statistics are interesting on food. For example, it is estimated that Americans throw away 40 percent of the food that is produced for U.S. consumption—20 pounds per person per month—worth a total of $165 million per year. See more details at www.behrmanhouse.com/universe.

- What is our inedible trash composed of? (*packaging; broken objects; inedible food waste such as peelings; disposable items such as tissues, napkins, paper towels, aluminum foil…*)
- What could be done to reduce the waste? (*Buy items that have less or no packaging or buy in bulk; learn how to repair stuff or find someone who does; use nondisposables as much as possible —e.g., cloth napkins, reusable storage containers instead of foil or plastic wrap.)*
- What are the main categories of unused objects and other items? (*things that were bought on a whim, unwanted gifts, clothing that has been outgrown or is out of fashion, etc.*)
- What could be done to reduce the waste? (*Think twice before impulse buying, give away unused items, find a different use for unwanted items.)*

Ask students what harm is caused by unnecessary consumption. Encourage them to fill in the checklist on page 46 in small groups, and then share their answers with the class. (*using up scarce resources to both manufacture and transport items; harming the environment through the disposal of excess waste [pollution caused by accumulated trash]; becoming a slave to stuff, where our possessions become more important than relationships, people, or values*)

2. A Waste-Free Ideal (15 minutes)

Ask students to read the passage on page 47 of the journal from the Midrash about how the date palm tree is a model of 100 percent usefulness.

Then ask students to think of other plants and animals that are or could be 100 percent usable, and to sketch them in their book. (*walnut and cherry trees, whose fruit and whose wood are very valuable; cows, which yield leather, meat, organs used for dog food, and ground-up bones for fertilizer*) Then think of examples of the opposite extreme, when an entire organism is "used up" just for one product. (*e.g., killing elephants for their tusks*)

Discuss:

- Were people more careful not to waste natural products when they were less technologically advanced? Why? (*They had to work harder to grow and make what they needed.*)
- Have the students consider their Waste Inventory. Did they throw out any items that they could have made use of? (*For example, you could give old clothes away to a thrift shop or use them as cleaning rags, you could compost food scraps or feed stale bread to the birds.)*
- Does being richer, and having a higher standard of living, lead to being more wasteful? Why? (*When we can afford to replace broken things, we're less motivated to repair them. When we are secure in our food sources, we're less careful to avoid wasting food.*)
- Are there things we routinely throw away that, if we thought about it, we could save and use? *(The seeds from pumpkins and watermelons can be toasted to make a healthy snack food; artists can reuse materials to make a statement about our lifestyle and beauty at the same time.)*

3. How Much Is Enough? (10 minutes)

Ask students to look at the three definitions of wealth from the Talmud on page 48 of their journals, choose the one they most agree with, and write down their thoughts on what would make them feel like they have enough, according to that definition. Ask students to share their responses with the class.

4. The Tenth Commandment (15 minutes)

Ask students to read together the commandment against coveting (Exodus 20:14) from page 49 of their journal. Discuss:

- What is the meaning of the word "covet"? (*to want something that belongs to another)*
- Why does the Torah forbid covetousness? (*perhaps because it might lead to theft, larceny, robbery, or simply bad relationships between people; perhaps because of the environmental impact of excessive materialism)*

Explain that in our consumer society, advertisements continually encourage us to consume more and more possessions, thereby increasing the amount of stuff we purchase. Discuss:

- How do advertisements encourage us to buy more stuff? (*They use catchy names and slogans, attractive models, freebies, and other techniques to make customers feel the product will improve their lives in some way.*)
- What positive effects does increased consumption have? (*More consumption means more products produced, more jobs created, and higher standards of living.)*
- What negative effects does increased consumption have? (*Increased consumption negatively impacts the environment through greater use of finite resources and more waste that needs to be disposed of; increased consumption may widen socioeconomic gaps; increased consumption makes us attach a lot of importance to material possessions instead of people and values or spiritual growth.)*
- Perhaps the solution lies in our ability to distinguish between things we **need** and things we **want** (and could do without).

Write two headings on the board, "Need" and "Want," and ask students to suggest examples of things they buy (or that are bought for them) because they need them versus things they buy because they want them. List the items below the headings. You can also delve deeper by asking about some "need" items, "How many of these do you *really* need, and how many do you want?"

Discuss: Where is the line between "need" and "want"? And is there anything wrong with buying something just because you want it? How much is too much?

Discuss: If people aren't able to control their own consumption, causing damage to themselves, others, and the environment, should governments or communities step in to try to prevent overconsumption, by law if necessary?

Enrichment Options

THE STORY OF STUFF The film *The Story of Stuff*, a popular 20-minute animation, presents an overview of the costs and benefits of consumption; show it to the class and discuss their impressions and questions. Find the link at www.behrmanhouse.com/universe.

Note: this film and a brief discussion of it can be used as either an opening or a concluding activity for the lesson. However, if you don't have time for it, you can recommend it for viewing at home by students and their families.

TRASH COMPETITION Have a competition among students to see who can produce the smallest amount of trash over a set period of time (three days, a week, etc.). Brainstorm with the class a list of ways to reduce waste (which may require them to involve their families!). Then, have them keep a trash journal, documenting every item that they throw away. At the end of the time period, students will present a description or an illustration of what went into their trash during the competition. Together students will judge the winner(s). This could then be translated into an educational campaign in the community, led by the students.

A PLACE FOR USED STUFF Look into whether there are secondhand stores or Freecycle groups in your area. Are students aware of them? Sponsor a community free-exchange day, when people bring items they don't need, in good condition, for others to take; what is left at the end of the day goes to a charity. Investigate and distribute a directory of resale shops in your area that accept used clothing and other items. Learn about the Freecycle Network at www.freecycle.org.

AD JOURNAL Suggest that students keep an ad journal for a day, counting and categorizing the ads they are exposed to on different media—billboards, TV, the Internet, magazines, etc. Are they surprised by how many ads they encounter in a day?

Lesson 11 — Climate Change

Central Question: How can we balance the needs and interests of the current inhabitants of earth with those of future generations?

Goals: Students will…

1. Explain in brief the standard scientific theory of climate change.
2. Reflect upon the dilemmas and the responsibilities imposed on us by climate change.
3. Define "renewable energy" and supply a few examples.

Introduction

In this lesson, students will explore the issue of climate change in depth, as a case study of a question of sustainable development. Since this is a complex issue that is currently perhaps the foremost environmental concern, we will devote a significant amount of time to making sure the students understand it thoroughly.

Global warming is a classic example of a dilemma in which the behavior of people living today (especially in the developed world) is changing the environment and may be having a significant negative impact on the lives of future generations (and even the present one). We will discuss why scientists' warnings are not heeded enough and study texts that shed some light on our responsibilities.

Materials Needed

Internet-connected computer and projector

Activities

1. Getting Started: What Is Climate Change? (15 minutes)

Show *Global Warming 101*, a 3-minute National Geographic video explaining the causes and effects of climate change (also known as global warming). Find the link on www.behrmanhouse.com/universe.

Ask students to match the terms and definitions in the journal on page 50.

Answers:

Greenhouse gases: Carbon dioxide, methane, and other gases that trap heat from the sun in the earth's atmosphere.

Fossil fuel: Oil, coal, and natural gas, formed in prehistoric times from plants that became buried in the earth. When burned as fuel, they release carbon dioxide and other gases.

The greenhouse effect: The process by which the sun's energy is reflected back to Earth by gases in the atmosphere, so it can't escape, and warms the Earth.

Climate change: A long-term change in the earth's average temperature, believed to be caused by gases created by human activity.

Then discuss the following to make sure students have understood the basic facts:

- How do we know that the earth is warming? (*a recent spate of warmer-than-average years and shrinking Arctic Sea ice)*
- What causes climate change? (*intensification of the greenhouse effect, brought on by the release of greenhouse gases from factories, power plants, and cars)*
- What is the name of one type of greenhouse gas? (*carbon dioxide, methane)*
- What are "fossil fuels"? *(fuels that come from decayed plant and animal matter, including oil, natural gas, and coal)*
- Besides warmer temperatures, how may global warming affect our lives? (*rising sea levels causing floods in coastal areas, higher frequency of hurricanes and droughts, species extinctions, populations living in low-lying areas will eventually need to relocate)*

2. Choni Sleeps for Seventy Years (20 minutes)

Explain that climate change is a long-term process, and we are now going to read and discuss a story about attitudes towards planning and acting for the future. Read the story of Choni, one of the sages of the Mishnah, in the journal (page 51). Discuss:

- Does the old man know the people who will eat the fruits of the tree he planted? Why is he working for their benefit? (*With the short lifespan in the ancient world, it is probable that the old man would not know any of the people who would eat the fruits of the tree. It seems he is repaying his moral debt to the previous generations who planted for him, by planting for the future.)*
- Do you think we should reserve all our efforts for the present generation or expend some effort to improve the lot of future generations? Why? What are the pros and cons? (*As the old man points out, we have a moral obligation to future generations, as a sort of repayment to the previous generations who took care of us—we pay back by paying forward. Some things can only be done for the future; if everyone were to think only of themselves, no one would ever invest in the far future. On the other hand, maybe our efforts will go to waste in the long run. Who knows if future generations will want carobs, or if there will be some environmental change that will kill carob trees, etc.)*
- How does this story apply to the issue of climate change? (*Climate change is an example of a situation in which people prefer to enjoy the short-term benefits of energy use, unlimited long-distance travel, etc., without giving sufficient thought to the effect on future generations.)*
- Why aren't people taking climate change more seriously? (*Some people are unaware of the long-term consequences; people may be more concerned with making a living for themselves and their families than with the needs of future generations; climate change is a slow process, and many believe that it may have catastrophic consequences only after their lives are over, so why pay a price in standard of living now; the problem can seem overwhelming, and our individual actions may seem ineffective compared to the scope of the problem; there is some controversy over the facts of climate change, so those in doubt may be reluctant to act.)*

3. Renewable Energy (15 minutes)

Read the opening two paragraphs (journal, page 52) with students and introduce the terms "sustainable development" (*providing for human needs while sustaining [preserving] resources and the environment for future generations*) and "renewable energy source" (*a source of energy that is continuously replenished and never [or at least not in our lifetime] runs out*).

Looking around us, there are many sustainable, renewable energy sources we could utilize to reduce our dependence on fossil fuels and our greenhouse gas emissions. Many natural phenomena that generate heat or motion can be harnessed to produce electricity.

Ask students, individually or in groups, to match the pictures of ancient and modern technologies to the renewable energy sources.

Answers: 1-d, 2-b, 3-a, 4-f, 5-h, 6-g, 7-c, 8-e

Ask students if they can think of other renewable energy sources. (*Some examples include tides, waves, effort of people and animals.)*

Point out that the choice of renewable energy sources depends on availability of resources. For example, you need a river to build a waterwheel. Discuss: What renewable energy resource is prevalent in your area? Do students know about any local large-scale projects that generate electricity?

Enrichment Options

GLOBAL EXPERIMENT You can demonstrate the physics of global warming using a simple experiment. Students can do it in class or at home. The experiment creates a small-scale simulation of the earth and its atmosphere, with or without the extra cover of greenhouse gases, and shows the difference in warming rate between the two conditions. Find the link to the experiment on www.behrmanhouse.com/universe.

THINK LOCAL Challenge students to find out how climate change is affecting your local town, city, or region. Have average temperatures risen over the years? Have weather patterns changed? Have there been more wildfires, tropical storms, or floods?

MAKING A CHANGE Help students, individually or as a class, write letters to people and organizations that can make changes to help reduce climate change—such as local farmers, manufacturers, local municipalities, school authorities, or parent organizations. Students might want to present themselves as members of a new generation, worried about how earlier generations are changing the world of their future. Suggest using the words of the old man from Choni's story (journal, page 51) to try to convince the addressees that they should think about future generations. As much as possible, students should offer concrete suggestions, such as installing a bike rack to encourage students to bike to school, replacing lightbulbs with the energy-saving kind, or organizing a "walking school bus." (see link on www.behrmanhouse.com/universe)

Lesson 12 — Large Tasks, Small Steps

Central Question: How can we make an impact on global issues when they seem too overwhelming?

Goals: Students will…

1. Explain how many of their daily activities contribute to global warming.
2. Develop skills to face seemingly overwhelming tasks (such as reducing global warming).

Introduction

In the previous lesson, we focused on the theory of global warming, looked at its causes and effects, and reflected on the situation in which people prefer to enjoy the short-term benefits of energy use, unlimited long-distance travel, and so on, at the possible cost of a future catastrophe. We will start this lesson by showing that many kinds of human activity contribute to global warming, so students can understand the magnitude of the task facing those who wish to slow the process.

Since the task might seem overwhelming, we will study a *midrash* about Rabbi Akiva that offers a strategy to deal with such situations: Don't feel responsible for the whole thing, it will only make you give up; instead, focus on what you can do, and do it. In this vein, we will conclude by creating posters to display in the school that suggest 10 ways individuals can reduce their carbon footprints.

Materials Needed

Poster boards, markers

Activities

1. Getting Started: Who, Me? Causes of Climate Change (15 minutes)

Ask students to look at the pictures in their journals (page 54) and write their thoughts about how each activity contributes to climate change. After a few minutes of individual work, discuss their answers as a class. Introduce some of the following ideas if students need help:

- **Watching TV:** *Manufacturing and transporting the TV requires the use of energy (burning fossil fuels, which releases carbon dioxide, a major "greenhouse gas" that causes the warming of the earth); running the TV requires electricity (usually produced by burning fossil fuels).*
- **Riding in a car:** *Manufacturing and transporting the car requires the use of energy (see above); conventional cars burn fossil fuels to run their engines, and this releases carbon dioxide.*
- **Eating a hamburger:** *Animals, particularly sheep and cattle, produce large amounts of methane, which is a greenhouse gas.*
- **Flying in an airplane:** *Jet airplanes emit huge amounts of greenhouse gases.*

Discuss with students their reactions to this activity. It seems that many—perhaps most—of our daily activities contribute to the warming of the earth. Multiply our own activities by all the billions of people around the world, and it may seem that there is no chance we can make a dent in the problem of climate change! (But don't despair, we will address this in the next activity.)

2. Small Steps (15 minutes)

An important reason why many people ignore the dangers of global warming is that they feel overwhelmed by the complexity of the issues and don't think that anything they do can have much effect on such a global phenomenon.

Ask the students to read and answer the questions in their journal at the top of page 55, including writing a paragraph or poem about a personal experience of giving up on a task that looked too daunting, or writing a letter to a real or fictional person facing a similarly hard task. Discuss what one can do in such situations, with a focus on breaking up the challenge into smaller steps and addressing them one by one.

Read together the story about Rabbi Akiva at the bottom of the page, and discuss what he learned from seeing how drops of water could carve stone:

- What examples of daunting, seemingly impossible tasks come to mind? (*Examples range from the mundane—tidying an extremely messy room or learning the material for a test—to ones of national or global importance— founding a Jewish state in a barren, sparsely populated land, or abolishing hunger worldwide.)*
- How can we apply Rabbi Akiva's realization to these kinds of challenges? (*Even the longest journey begins with one step. You have to be willing to take that step in order to get anywhere.)*

Rabbi Akiva's experience encourages every one of us to take responsibility and try to do as much as is in our power to work for a better world. Knowing that even the smallest actions can make a difference encourages us not to walk away from global challenges. This is an application of the Jewish concept of *tikun olam*, a mitzvah that literally means "repairing the world"— a task incumbent upon every Jew.

3. Tikun Olam (20 minutes)

Discuss with students how the issue of climate change is particularly appropriate for application of the concept of *tikun olam*, repairing the world. It seems that we humans, unwittingly, have built a civilization with the power to actually change the climate of our planet for the worse. Therefore it is our responsibility to find ways to repair the damage we have done, because, as we have seen in previous lessons, the earth is not ours alone; it belongs to all species and to future generations.

Assign students to work in small groups to create posters for the school that will recommend 10 simple things every student can do to reduce greenhouse gases and combat global warming. Display the posters in the school corridors or common areas, if possible. Students can use their personal knowledge, research the Internet, or use material you provide from www.behrmanhouse.com/universe.

Encourage students to choose one item from their posters and commit to carrying it out. You might create a chart on which they could report their success in keeping their commitment each week. Or have the whole class pick one item each week for everyone to work on.

Additional options:

- Submit the posters, or a class list of *tikun olam* ideas, to the synagogue bulletin.
- Organize a visit by the rabbi to discuss climate change.
- Organize a meeting with the synagogue director to discuss ways to reduce the carbon footprint of the building.

Enrichment Options

PUZZLE TIME: WORD TRAIN If students have time, challenge them to solve the puzzle in the journal, page 57.

Answers:
1. lightbulb
2. bus
3. shower
4. rechargeable
5. electric
6. compost
7. tree

PROJECT BASED LEARNING: GREENING THE SYNAGOGUE Have students research ideas for reducing the carbon footprint of the synagogue. They might research such topics as insulation, solar energy, passive cooling, and geothermal heating/cooling. They could interview a green architect or engineer. Then students or teams could produce sketches or written proposals showing how the synagogue could set an example in using technology to reduce greenhouse gas emissions.

Using student-driven goals and a real-life presentation, craft a project based learning activity around this topic. See page 64 for more information on project based learning, and also visit www.behrmanhouse.com/project-based-learning.

Further Resources

Visit www.behrmanhouse.com/universe for more resources and motivating articles about facing large tasks by taking small steps.

CHAPTER

6

Setting Limits

It's part of human nature to investigate the world and to use our learning to try to improve our world. But what are the limits, if any, on the right of humans to intervene in the very processes of nature? Should our decisions be based purely on cost-benefit calculations and risk assessment, or is there a religious—or moral—question to be considered? Lessons 13 and 14 explore two case studies involving major manipulations of natural processes for (hopefully) human benefit: genetic engineering and nuclear energy.

Please note: This chapter contains advanced topics that raise difficult philosophical and practical questions. Give students plenty of time for questions and to express their fears or other strong feelings. If possible, invite the rabbi or an expert in these fields to come speak with the class about these issues. If the available course time is not sufficient for this, you might want to skip ahead to chapter 7.

As an introduction to this chapter, invite students to journal their thoughts about making changes to the natural world (journal, page 58).

Lesson 13 — Genetic Engineering: Are We Playing God?

Central Questions: What are the ethics of technological advances that change the way natural processes work? Is it okay for such technologies to be used carefully and responsibly, or is the very technology too risky or inherently wrong?

Goals: Students will...

1. Define genetic engineering and explain why it's controversial.
2. Explain how insights from Jewish sources can help us in our thinking about the dilemmas involved in genetic engineering.

Introduction

Advances in biotechnology have given us the ability to manipulate life forms in ways that not long ago were the subject of science fiction. It seems that there will soon be no aspect of life that we cannot modify or even create. Organ transplants, genetic engineering, artificial organs, cloning... As we break down the technological limits to our interventions in life, we need to ask if there are moral or religious limits. Are there interventions that we should not do, no matter what the benefits?

In this lesson we'll examine one controversial example, genetic engineering, using it as a case study to consider questions of whether and how to limit human intervention in nature. Genetic engineering is the manipulation of the characteristics of an organism by "transplanting" into it genes from a different organism, maybe even from a different species altogether, thus creating something that could not have arisen in nature.

Activities

1. Getting Started: Creating New Life Forms (15 minutes)

Ask students to read the paragraph in their journals about crossbreeding (page 59). Explain that new technologies open up the possibilities for creating new organisms that combine the characteristics of different species.

Have the students imagine and draw their own creative combinations of organisms in the space provided in their journals. Remind them to think about the benefits (and risks) that each new animal or plant offers. There is the temptation to be silly in this activity, but remind students that our goal is to create organisms for a purpose, to benefit people or the world.

Let students present their inventions to the class. Then discuss:

- What benefits might such new combinations provide? (*They might help address problems of world hunger, water shortage, disease, energy shortage, global warming, pollution, etc.*)
- What risks might such creativity involve? (*Unexpected consequences due to characteristics we didn't plan or expect; for example, a new organism might be so strong and successful at reproduction that it would crowd out or eat other useful organisms.*)
- Is there a moral limit to such manipulations, regardless of practical consequences?

2. Must We Leave Nature Alone? (10 minutes)

Jewish sources suggest two opposing views regarding intervention in nature, which are presented in the two texts given in the journal, page 60. Ask students to explain these views in their own words.

(Nachmanides says God made a perfect world, and it is not for us to tamper with it. The division into species is not accidental, but part of a plan, and we can never know enough, as humans, to be sure that our tampering with the system will not cause catastrophe in the future. However, according to Otzar Hamidrashim, *humans have the powers to improve the world—curing diseases, producing food, building shelter, creating culture. It is not reasonable to assume that we were supposed to remain cavemen, forever hunting and gathering and dying young.)*

Discuss students' responses to these two opposing views. Point out that while the second position may seem obvious in regard to advances in curing disease and plowing fields, when we think about technologies for cloning humans, we find ourselves struggling to figure out where to draw a line. You might suggest an escalating set of questions, to see if students can agree on where to draw the line. For example: Is it all right to...

- Use vaccines to completely wipe out smallpox virus from the world?
- Culture cells from cows, to grow large quantities of meat in tanks in a factory?
- Perform face transplants?
- Perform brain transplants?
- Create a new species by implanting genes for great size and strength from a gorilla into a human embryo?
- Make clones of humans, by taking a few cells from a person and growing them into an entire person who would be an identical twin (only younger)?

3. Genetic Engineering (20 minutes)

Today, we can take a gene from one organism and insert it in another, without crossbreeding. This is called genetic engineering, and the results of these gene manipulations are called GMOs, genetically modified organisms. The journal contains a case study on page 61, with suggested arguments pro and con. Ask students to work in small groups (or in whole-class discussion) to evaluate the pros and cons of genetically modified corn, a currently controversial issue.

Or divide the class in half and conduct a debate with one side presenting the pros and the other the cons of GMOs. Give students 5 minutes to prepare their arguments. Allow 2 to 3 minutes for opening arguments and 2 to 3 minutes for rebuttals.

4. Should There Be Rules? Limits? (5 minutes)

Lead a discussion about whether there should be rules governing genetic engineering. Who gets to decide which kinds of genetic engineering are allowed? (*businesses, scientific community, government, United Nations?*) Could such rules be enforced?

Enrichment Options

BIOENGINEERING REPORT Suggest that individuals or groups of students research other examples of bioengineering and prepare a report or poster describing the pros and cons. For example: cloning, artificial organs, organ transplants. Their presentation should also include their understanding of how the Jewish texts we studied in this lesson relate to the issue at hand.

SCI-FI VISION: Ask students who are interested in science fiction to look back at books and movies they like, and see what visions the authors present regarding the potential, and the problems, of modifying biology, human or otherwise. They can then make presentations to the class, with slides or film clips.

Further Resources

Visit www.behrmanhouse.com/universe for more resources about genetic engineering and the controversy surrounding it, suggestions for classroom science experiments that examine the effects of genetic engineering, and more.

Lesson 14 — Nuclear Energy: Evaluating Risks

Central Questions: How much risk can we tolerate? Are there activities that humans should avoid, despite the benefits, because the risks are too great?

Goals: Students will…

1. Recognize the pros and cons of nuclear power production.
2. Reflect on the moral dilemma presented by humankind's newfound ability to tamper with fundamental natural phenomena.
3. Learn how Jewish sources from the past can give us insight to deal with our current concerns.

Introduction

Few technologies illustrate the dilemma between benefit and risk as intensely as does nuclear power generation. Viewed by some as the ultimate "green" energy source, emitting minimal pollution and requiring only small amounts of natural resources, it terrifies others in its potential to cause catastrophe. It is a powerful example of the complicated dilemmas posed by man's tampering with nature.

Albert Einstein once said: "The discovery of nuclear chain reactions need not bring about the destruction of mankind any more than did the discovery of matches. We only must do everything in our power to safeguard against its abuse." Whether or not that is within our power, and whether we are willing to live with that risk, is the driving force behind this dilemma.

Activities

1. Getting Started: The Golem of Prague (25 minutes)

Assign students to read the story "The Golem of Prague," on page 62 of the journal, either independently or together as a class.

Discuss:

- Why did the rabbi create the golem? Do you think he was justified in doing so? *(Few people could resist the temptation to create a golem that would miraculously solve their problems and the problems of their community. Given the powerlessness of Jews in Eastern Europe at the time, this impulse is even more understandable. From a position of utter powerlessness, the Jewish community is empowered by the creation of the golem.)*
- Should the rabbi have consulted with the other members of the community before deciding to create a golem? *(When a whole community might be seriously affected by a decision, they should be asked what they think.)*
- Why did the rabbi's wife object to the creation of the golem? Do you think it is a sin to create a living creature? *(The rabbi's wife seems to have had two reservations: creating a living creature seemed to her an act of hubris, a sin; she was fearful of the unforeseen consequences.)*

- What would have happened had the rabbi not managed to erase the letter from the golem's forehead? (*Judging by the golem's brief rampage, catastrophe could have resulted, with the Golem traveling far and wide strewing destruction in its path. What started out as a local phenomenon could have destroyed the whole world.)*
- Can you imagine any circumstances in which the rabbi might have decided to reanimate the golem, notwithstanding the risks? (*One could envision drastic situations, such as during the Holocaust.)*

Ask students if they could create such a creature, would they? Why or why not? If time permits, let students draw their creature, imagining what it would look like and what it could do.

2. What Is Nuclear Energy? (25 minutes)

We will now discuss an example of a human-created technology that has the potential for going seriously out of control: nuclear energy. Invite students to suggest benefits and costs or risks of nuclear energy, or fill out the chart in their journals, page 63.

Answers might include:
Benefits:

- Nuclear energy does not use up resources.
- It is essentially limitless, and so can eliminate our dependency on oil, gas, and coal.
- It does not generate carbon dioxide (a major component of the greenhouse gases causing global warming).
- It does not generate smoke or noise pollution.

Risks:

- There is a danger of radiation pollution to air, water, soil, crops.
- It creates radioactive wastes, which are difficult to store safely and will last forever.
- There's a risk of catastrophe (like the meltdowns in Chernobyl, Russia, in 1986, and in Fukushima, Japan, in 2011).
- The technology could be subverted to create extremely destructive weapons.

The story of the golem raises many dilemmas that are relevant to a discussion of nuclear energy:

- How is the story of the golem related to nuclear energy? *(The story of the golem is a premodern fable about technology running out of control, about man tampering with the foundations of nature and creating a monster that could potentially alter the whole world. There are parallels between the story and the technology of nuclear power generation: a person/people who has/have the dangerous knowledge to create a powerful creature, which can do much for the good of the whole community but also with the potential for massive destruction.)*
- Who should be involved in the decision whether to build a nuclear reactor, since potentially it can have such far-reaching effects? (*Accidents that have occurred so far in nuclear reactors around the world have sometimes had effects that went beyond political boundaries. Arguably, nuclear energy production should be governed by an international body, perhaps the United Nations, so as to grant a say to all people who may be affected by the technology.)*

- Are there technologies that we can use but should refrain from using, since we would risk making changes in the world that we might only discover when it was too late to undo them? (*Nuclear energy is one example, along with genetic engineering [see previous lesson]. Other examples of potential modern golems might include cloning, bionic people, or intelligent robots.*)

Enrichment Options

NUCLEAR POWER PLANT Suggest that students find out if there is a nuclear power plant in their area. If not, where is the closest one? How much electricity does it produce? How many households does this provide for? Can they go on a visit to the plant?

CHAPTER

7

Striking the Right Balance

It seems that finding the right place for ourselves in the natural world is not a question of choosing between simple, black-and-white alternatives, but rather an ongoing, complex, and even confusing exploration of costs and benefits to ourselves and to the world. In this chapter, lesson 15 presents a classic case study of human intervention in nature—the famous project of draining the Hula swamp in Israel—that seemed at the time obviously a good idea, but which turned out in retrospect to be a bad idea. So maybe the main message is: Go slow, and be humble. Lesson 16 encourages students to see how they can make a difference for the environment and provides examples of Jewish initiatives that strive to make a difference. Lesson 17 offers students the opportunity to articulate a set of guidelines for our time, for defining our relationship to the natural universe.

As an introduction to this chapter, invite students to journal their thoughts, questions, and conclusions about this course on page 64 of the journal.

Lesson 15 — The Hula Valley: The Law of Unintended Consequences

Central Question: What is our responsibility to the environment when our actions may have unforeseen effects on nature?

Goals: Students will…

1. Examine a large-scale case of human intervention in nature, in Israel.
2. Define the law of unintended consequences, the idea that it is sometimes impossible to foresee all the effects of human intervention in a natural system.
3. Reflect upon humanity's responsibility to do no harm to the environment.

Introduction

In this lesson we will explore in detail one example of large-scale human intervention in a natural habitat: the draining of the swamps in Israel's Hula valley in the 1950s. In the first flush of its glory as a newly independent state, inundated by a massive influx of immigrants who needed food and work, Israel embarked upon this project, determined to conquer nature and impose the nation's will upon it. The project had much appeal. Draining the swamps would create fertile new farmland, eliminate malaria, promote the Zionist ideal of working the land, and offer a large-scale enterprise to enlist the energies of the young country and bring its diverse population together. It became a symbol to the whole Jewish world of the Israeli pioneer spirit and ambition, and *tikun olam.*

The environmental consequences of the project were not foreseen at the time, but eventually they became all too apparent: several native species became extinct, soil and water quality in the area deteriorated, and migration patterns were disturbed. Parts of the valley have since been reflooded, in an attempt to partially roll back the drainage project; indeed part of the swamp has been restored to a very popular nature preserve that attracts migrating birds—and curious tourists—by the thousands. The story offers a cautionary tale of the impact that human intervention can have upon sensitive habitats.

Materials Needed

Internet-connected computer and projector, Consequence Cards (downloaded from www.behrmanhouse.com/universe)

Advance Preparation: Print the Consequence Cards from www.behrmanhouse.com/universe and cut them out.

Activities

1. Getting Started: A Flock of Birds (10 minutes)

Ask for a volunteer to read aloud the story in the journal, page 65. Students should then answer the questions.

Explain that this story is an example of the law of unintended consequences, which says that an intervention in a complex system usually creates unanticipated and often undesirable outcomes. Ask students to think of examples from their own experience.

2. Draining the Hula (15 minutes)

Show students the Jewish National Fund movie describing the draining of the swamps in the Hula valley. You can find the link at www.behrmanhouse.com/universe. (Watch until minute 7:00, or stop sooner if attention flags.)

Discuss the following questions:

- What benefits were expected by the draining of the Hula? *(eradication of malaria; creation of much-needed new farmland, because arable land in Israel is quite limited)*
- Was the project, as described in the film, a success? *(Yes!)*
- If you were planning such a project, what unintended consequences would you be worried about? *(It may be unfair to ask this question in hindsight, but we now know that meddling in complex wetland ecosystems is hazardous, with wide-reaching effects on water, soil, and animal and plant species. We will examine these effects in detail in the next part of the lesson.)*
- Remind the students of the film's opening statement: "This is the story of the Hula valley, the story of the eternal struggle between man and nature, between civilization and wilderness…." Ask: What do you think about this worldview? Can you think of alternative worldviews?

3. And the Results? (15 minutes)

Spread the Consequence Cards (see Materials) on the floor or on tables or desks all around the room. Divide the students into four teams. Assign a topic to each team, and write the topics on the board:

- Water quality
- Animal species
- Bird migration
- Soil quality

Explain that each card has a sentence about the draining of the Hula valley swamp that relates to one of the four topics. There are three cards for each topic, and when assembled, they will each make a cohesive paragraph. Students should wander around the room and collect all the cards that belong to their topic, and then assemble their paragraph. They can take notes in the journal, page 66.

When all paragraphs have been assembled, each team should explain to the class the consequences of the Hula drainage project on their assigned topic.

For reference, here are the assembled paragraphs for each topic:

> **Water quality:** When Hula Lake still stood, the water flowing from Mount Hermon into Lake Kinneret (Sea of Galilee) made its way slowly through the swampy Hula valley. The valley served as a huge filtering system, with debris carried by the water sinking down to the lakebed, leaving the water to flow more cleanly into the Kinneret. When Hula Lake was drained, canals were built to funnel the water

quickly across the valley, with the unintended result that it carried the debris along with it, polluting the Kinneret, a major source of drinking water for Israel.

Animal species: Research has shown that hundreds of species of animals lived in the Hula valley before the drainage project. These animals included insects, crustaceans, snails, clams, fish, amphibians, reptiles, birds, and mammals. When the valley was drained, many of these creatures' habitats were destroyed, and several species became extinct.

Bird migration: The Hula valley is a major stop in the route used by birds migrating between Europe and Africa. The birds travel thousands of miles in an exhausting and dangerous journey to greener pastures. In the autumn, millions of birds make their way south to Africa, escaping the harsh European winters. In the spring, the birds return to Europe to nest and raise their young. When the valley was drained, the migrating birds had to find alternative places to rest and find food and water along their journeys. This made their trip much harder.

Soil quality: The ground under the lake and swamp was a layer of peat, decayed plant matter kept continuously wet by the water covering it. When the water was drained, the peat dried and changed its characteristics. The top layers of dried peat crumbled into black, fine-grained dust, which the winds blew onto the neighboring fields, covering the crops. Large underground caverns formed in the peat, sometimes collapsing without warning. The dried peat fueled smoldering underground fires, which sometimes burned for months on end and were extremely difficult to extinguish.

Tell the students that part of the Hula valley was reflooded, creating a haven for migrating birds. The resulting oasis serves as a center for ecotourism, with people coming from all over the world to enjoy the migrating birds. You can refer the students to impressive videos that show huge flocks of migrating cranes in the valley (see Further Resources below).

4. Unintended Consequences Revisited (10 minutes)

Ask the students to try to predict the consequence or consequences for each event in the chart in the journal, page 67, then review together and see how they've done. What are their conclusions about the possibility of foreseeing the effects of human intervention on the environment?

The exercise demonstrates the far-reaching and unexpected effects caused by various actions. Nowadays, most large-scale infrastructure projects in the developed world require environmental impact assessments to be carried out before commencing work, but these are often no guarantee against unforeseen effects.

5. Human Responsibility (5 minutes — optional)

If time allows, ask students to read the *midrash* in the journal, page 67.

Discuss: Why does God put extra responsibility on humanity, as opposed to the other animals? (*Humanity is very powerful and has a much larger effect on the environment than any other animal. And humans are conscious beings, aware of the consequences of their actions and capable of taking on responsibility.)*

Enrichment Options

FURTHER INVESTIGATION Working in small groups, students can choose one of the consequences of the draining of the Hula valley, described briefly in the lesson, and investigate it further, creating a presentation that shows maps, studies, pictures, and more. Another option is for students to look for information about wetland drainage and/or conservation projects in their area. And a third direction would be to research other examples of similar cases of unintended consequences (e.g., the dust bowl in the 1930s, the importing of rabbits to Australia, the effects of beach development on the New Jersey shore).

Further Resources

Visit www.behrmanhouse.com/universe for more information about environmental issues in Israel today, the cranes in the Hula valley, and an online game that explores ecosystems.

Lesson 16 — Innovation and Inspiration

Central Questions: How can I as an individual or as part of a small community have any influence over global environmental concerns? How can we change the way society thinks and behaves?

Goals: Students will…

1. Give examples of specific actions they can take themselves to make an impact on global environmental issues.
2. Be familiar with examples of Jewish environmental initiatives in North America and Israel.

Introduction

As we have seen in previous lessons, human activity on the planet has wide-ranging effects on the environment. This was already understood in biblical times, and as we have seen, the Torah contains several commandments that try to hold the balance between the human need to exploit natural resources and the value of preserving the environment. Thus, Jewish teachings can provide us with guidance as to how to view our place in the universe; however, at times the challenges can seem overwhelming, and it may feel like we cannot really make a difference or have any effect on complex worldwide issues. In this lesson we will look at various examples of Jewish initiatives that strive to make a difference.

Materials Needed

Internet-connected computer, projector for viewing film clip; copy of the book *The Lorax*, by Dr. Seuss (Random House, 1971); poster board, magic markers; printouts of Sde Eliyahu products (optional)

Activities

1. Getting Started: The Lorax's Message (20 minutes)

Watch the trailer for the movie *Dr. Seuss' The Lorax* together.

Ask someone in the class to summarize the story for anyone who doesn't know it, or read the brief summary in the journal, page 68. Read the last few lines of the book *The Lorax* together.

Discuss the question of taking personal responsibility for the environment. Have students write their ideas for ways they could have intervened to prevent the sad ending of the story, and then compare their responses. (*Ideas might include: demonstrate against the Once-ler's activities, boycott his products, invent a way to make thneeds without Truffula trees, make a law requiring the Once-ler to plant a new tree for every tree he cuts down, require people to recycle their used thneeds, create a genetically modified Truffula that regrows when it is cut down, learn to live without thneeds, place a very high tax on thneeds.)*

Discuss how such actions fall into two categories:

1. Large-scale policy changes/actions by those in power (for example, the Kyoto treaty, a United Nations

agreement to reduce greenhouse gases; outlawing Freon gas; building regional plants to recycle waste water; financing studies to create clean energy sources).

2. Small changes by a lot of people (such as reducing the use of plastic shopping bags, using water and electricity responsibly, recycling, switching to bikes for local transportation, using public transportation).

Discuss: How can we as individuals help with the first action? How can we help with the second action? What would have been the most effective and realistic action we could have taken to prevent the disaster in *The Lorax?* Are there current examples of problems where our actions could have impact?

Jews around the world are seeking new ways to change the world we live in by creating frameworks to raise awareness, develop new paradigms of behavior, innovate "greener" technologies, and build new communities dedicated to a Judaism that is in tune with nature.

The next two activities take a closer look at two initiatives, one in the United States and one in Israel, one social and the other commercial.

2. Environmental Initiatives: Hazon (10 minutes)

Divide the class into pairs or small groups with access to computers. Have them go online, look up Hazon, and explore its website. Hazon is a nonprofit organization that promotes creating healthier and more sustainable communities in the Jewish world and beyond.

Ask them to choose one program, out of the various initiatives offered on the site, that they would be most interested in joining and answer the questions found in their journal (page 69).

Discuss the questions together. You can take a vote to see which is the most popular activity and try to answer the questions for it.

3. Environmental Initiatives: Kibbutz Sde Eliyahu (15 minutes)

You may want to open this section with an introduction about *kibbutzim* in general and Sde Eliyahu in particular (for information visit www.behrmanhouse.com/universe).

Divide the class into small groups; assign each group to review the article about the kibbutz via the link on www.behrmanhouse.com/universe, and choose one sustainable development project. Each group should study its project and then design an advertisement to "sell" the product or technique. They can sketch the ad in their journals (page 69), draw it on a large poster, or devise a commercial to perform for the class.

Give students 10 minutes to prepare, and then have the different groups present their advertisements to the rest of the class.

4. Wrap-Up (5 minutes)

Read the passage from *Pirkei Avot 2:21* in the journal, page 69. Ask the class to rephrase it in their own words or to tell what this teaching means to them, and to give examples of what Rabbi Tarfon might have meant.

Discuss why this advice is particularly relevant to global environmental problems whose solutions require the cooperation of governments and industries. Whole societies have to change. This might make us feel that there is nothing we can do as individuals to make a difference. Rabbi Tarfon teaches that even if we have no chance of completing the task, we must still try, we must still do what we can—and by doing that, we show others the way.

Enrichment Options

GET INVOLVED Organize local participation in a Hazon project, or organize a field trip to a Jewish environmental education center like those listed on the website.

Further Resources

Visit www.behrmanhouse.com/universe for links to *The Lorax* trailer, information about *kibbutzim* and sustainable development, Hazon, Sde Eliyahu, and other environmental organizations, including the Earth Charter Initiative, Kibbutz Lotan, Isabella Freedman, and the Jewish Farm School.

Lesson 17 —From Knowledge to Action

Central Question: What do we take with us from the course that will affect our daily lives?

Goals: Students will…

1. Look back on the course and review some of the things they've learned.

2. Make the leap from knowledge to action.

Introduction

Throughout this course we have attempted to familiarize students with a wide range of concepts and ideas, framing a Jewish approach to environmentalism. In this lesson we will summarize our learning so far, and then encourage students to advance from learning to action by framing a Ten Commandments for the Environment.

Materials Needed

Whiteboard and markers, Bibles (enough copies for students to share), Post-it Notes (about 10 for each student), poster board, markers, glue, scissors

Advance Preparation: You may want to prepare the classroom in advance, hanging products of the previous lessons (collages, posters, stories, and drawings) on the walls to remind the students of the road they've traveled.

Activities

1. Getting Started: Where Do We Go from Here? (15 minutes)

Ask the students: What have you learned in this course? What concepts, stories, principles, and teachings do you remember? Students should spend five minutes writing their thoughts in their journals (page 70). Then ask for volunteers to share, and write their items on the board. The board now represents the knowledge that we have gained during this course. Now for the next step, from knowledge to action.

Explain that while knowledge is very important in Judaism (witness the importance of the mitzvah of Talmud Torah, studying the Torah and all the writings based on it), it is not an end in itself. The Talmud (*Kiddushin* 40b) says that "study is greater than action because it leads to action." This is a fundamental Jewish principle, that our deeds and actions are crucial. This is why Judaism spends so much time, effort, and words on detailed laws that guide us in our everyday lives.

Ask the students to write in their journals any changes they have made in their actions as a result of something they learned in this class.

2. The Ten Commandments (5 minutes)

The world has changed in recent centuries; rapid technological advancements have had a large impact on our world. Perhaps it is time to add a new section to *halachah*, Jewish law, specifying how we should behave to balance mastery of the natural world (Genesis 1) with tending it (Genesis 2). Before we do that, we'll take a look at what is perhaps the most important set of laws that Judaism has given the world, as an exercise toward framing our laws.

Ask the students to read the Ten Commandments in the Torah (Exodus 20:1-14). Examine the characteristics of the commandments, using the following questions:

- Which ones are phrased positively? Negatively?
- Which ones give detail? Why?
- Which ones explain the reasons behind them? Why?
- Which ones promise a reward? Why?

Discuss: Which of these characteristics, in your opinion, make a commandment most effective? The commandments were engraved on stone tablets. In today's era of massive ad campaigns, how would they look?

3. Ten Commandments for the Environment (30 minutes)

Divide the class into small groups, and supply each group with Post-it Notes. Each group should proceed with the steps laid out in their journals (page 71) to brainstorm and create their own "Ten Commandments for the Environment." Plan on having groups spend 15 minutes brainstorming their list of commandments.

Then distribute poster board and supplies to each group and ask them to make a poster of their own "10 Commandments for the Environment" tablets. Give them 10 minutes to complete their posters.

At the end of the session, reserve some time for students to present their posters. If you like, you can challenge them to commit to keeping their own commandments, by writing them in their journals, page 71, and signing the formal declaration on that page.

Enrichment Options

MEASURING PROGRESS Suggest that students pick one of their commandments and resolve to follow it as much as they can for the coming month. Students should think about how they can measure and quantify their progress, and prepare a report at the end of the month showing how they did. Examples include: weighing the amount of trash the family generates, counting miles traveled by bus/bike/foot/car, recording water consumption.

Project Based Learning

What Is Project Based Learning?

Project Based Learning (PBL) is a teaching strategy that enriches student learning through inquiry. It begins with a driving question — an authentic query about a meaningful topic for students—and ends with learners presenting the results of their work in a public forum, often in a venue other than the classroom. Because PBL gives students a voice in the learning process and capitalizes on their natural desire to learn, it holds special promise for both Jewish and environmental education. When properly implemented, project based learning activities will enable students to acquire a deeper understanding of and make personal connections to their Jewish heritage.

Implementing Project Based Learning: Seven Easy Steps

1. The teacher identifies a content area for the project and goals and objectives to be achieved.
2. The teacher develops a driving question that focuses the project and has authentic meaning for the students.
3. Students generate questions they will need to answer in order to solve the problem.
4. With input from students, the teacher creates a timeline for the project and communicates it to students and parents.
5. Students research answers to the questions, reading textbooks and newspapers, searching online resources, conducting interviews, taking field trips, etc. Learning happens at school and/or at home.
6. Teachers and students continually reflect on and evaluate the learning process, while they're working on the project and also when it's completed.
7. Students present their results in a public venue, such as a school assembly, a museum exhibit, a newspaper article, a web page, or even a community garden. Presentations might include written work, artwork, video, photos, or even an experiment or demonstration of a natural phenomenon or a technology (e.g., a simulation of global warming; a self-contained ecosystem [terrarium]; or a device that saves water, electricity, or heat).

Using Project Based Learning for *Our Place in the Universe*

The Enrichment Options at the end of many of the lessons in this book include ideas for project based learning activities that will help students explore their relationship with the natural world and develop a Jewish response to environmental issues. You can create an authentic, meaningful project based learning experience by following the steps above.

You may find a graphic organizer to be a useful tool for organizing the project. You can find a blank template on www.behrmanhouse.com/universe. Also, consider using the Online Learning Center, where students can share research with group members, blog about issues related to the project, and even present the final project.